COFFEE DRINKERS MAKE BETTER LOVERS

Other eBooks by Melvin Tan

LOVE & LOSS: A survivor's Instagram poetry

100 #SIXWORDSTORY

语录: Instagram 散文创作

断句中的俳句
A Collection of Chinese Haiku

Follow @rainy_day_survivor on Instagram for more.

COFFEE DRINKERS MAKE BETTER LOVERS

A Stroke Memoir

Melvin Tan

Copyright © 2019 by Melvin Tan.

ISBN:
Softcover
978-981-11-1732-9

Cover design by Jeffrey Mooi.
Back cover photo by Leon Isaac Lim.
Typesetting by Meow Ling.

CONTENTS

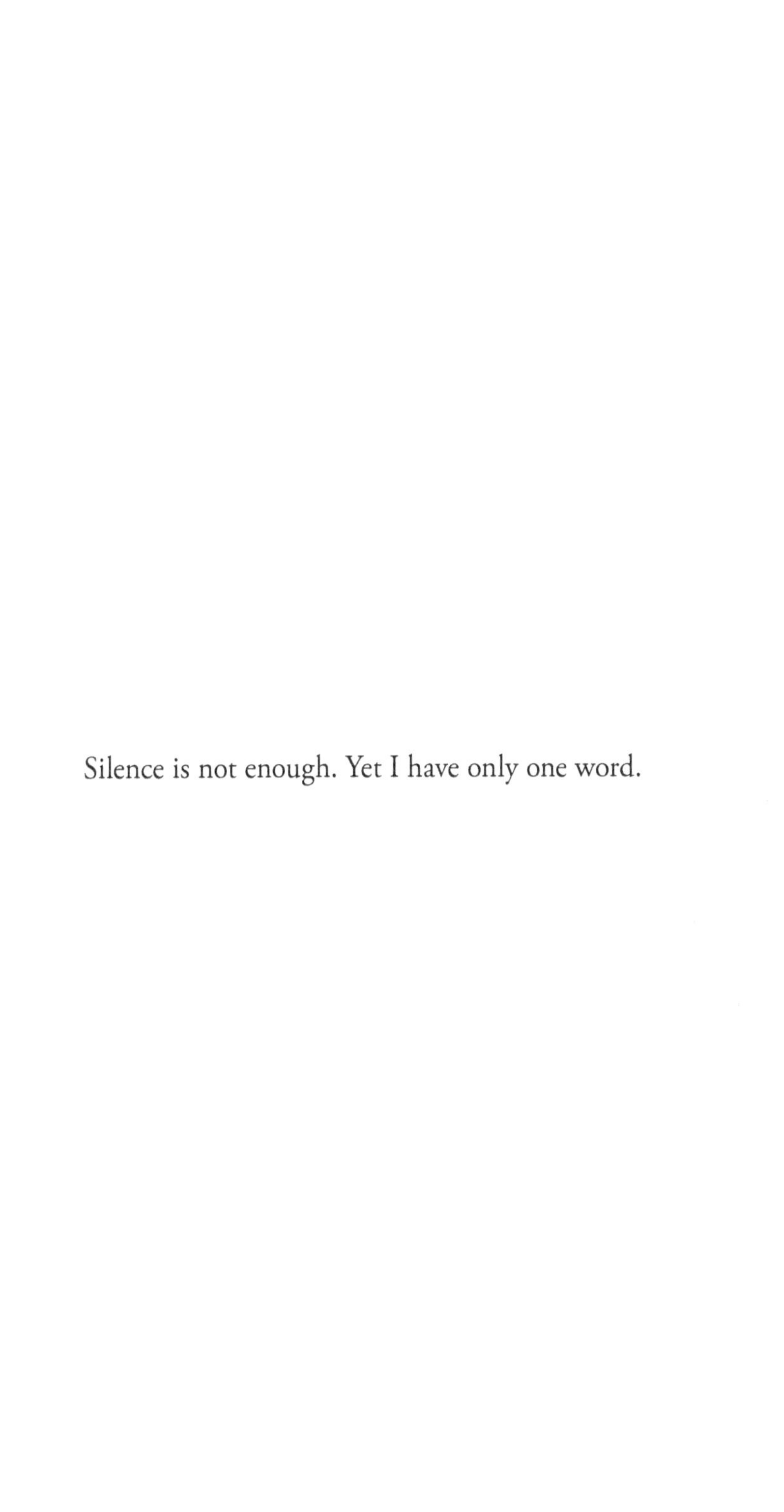

Silence is not enough. Yet I have only one word.

Thanks.

AROMA
Boy-meets-girl on Instagram

1

Love can't be found. It happens.
15 Jan 2011

See you tomorrow, came her reply with a sparkle and heart.

I reached over my head and swiveled a quick eye, taking in the room with a deep draw. Peace. Save for my pesky nephew outside.

Oh well, see you soon.

Insta-what? A buddy—an Apple Jedi—had told me about a new app on the block. It is a social photo-sharing app hitting the sweet spot between Hipstamatic and Facebook. It might turn out to be a dud but best to grab while it is free. I could find it easily on the App Store but sometimes I like to make life harder for myself. Life is more interesting that way, letting forgetfulness gnaw bit by bit. That's it! *Instagram.*

On the way to work, I pulled up the app. It is already racking up a bunch of followers who call themselves IGers. Looks fun. I set it aside for more play after work. During lunch, I whipped out my phone and hit the app again. The simple interface nailed it. I became an IGer and began tinkering.

I refreshed the *Popular* page again to look for interesting people to follow. People with the Zakka aesthetic. Or Scandinavian minimalism. Or poignant photo quotes. I did not follow people who post photos taken with a SLR. That defeats the spur-of-the-moment spirit of mobile photography. It amazes me how photographers compose their shots. Rule of Third. Leading lines. Scale. Framing. All decided in a single moment. The moment of now or never. Aik Beng Chia aka ABC would become a famous Singapore IGer. His snapshots of everyday life were my favorite. Back then, ABC only shot with his phone or a point-and-shoot. You do not need a 'real' camera to capture real emotions. The grit. The rawness. Poetry in action.

But this dude was different.

He obviously shot on an SLR. There was something about his photos, though. For one, instead of the obligatory 'golden hour' beachscape, there was a tight violent surge. He was just different. I 'followed' him and tapped the heart icon on many of his photos. One evening my phone chimed. It is that photography buff. He had 'liked' my photos. I like my posts to be juxtaposed shots with thoughtful captions and life quotes. And of course, Instagram-worthy cafe grub. He commented on one and soon, we ended up 'talking' on *Instagram*. He turned out to be a 'she' (duh). 'Likes' aflutter soon became *like*. We 'talked' so much that we steered our chats from *Instagram* to *WhatsApp*. Just seeing that her *Last Seen Today* timing was our chat together made me go all silly. I suppose this is how flirting with a pen pal starts before the digital gee-whiz came along.

With such a *duh* handle, I never guessed it belonged to a Chinese girl living in Japan. I told my colleagues Sonia and I met through friends to evade scrutiny. I saw how they interrogated another friend. It is clear they have never heard of the Geneva Conventions. Reporting my rank and name is not going to save my ass. I had to think of something quick. How am I going to explain this? One thing led to another, I cannot imagine a nonchalant download of an app will lead to this. If this is not a dream come true, I do not know what is. But I know I wanted excitement in life.

Don't we all?

***

Why did you use hearts with him. Sullen words prodded.
They don't mean anything.
Then do we mean anything, I punched in.

Welcome to emoji-verse. The Japanese have been texting emoticons since the 90s so Sonia got a head-start. Technology bridges physical distance but isolates because it sorely lacks one thing. Touch. Emoticons can hardly convey tone with no body language. The *Couple* app gets

around this with a "thumb kiss". The phone vibrates when
both users touch it in the same spot, real-time. That soon
became a game of *Kiss or Miss.* Sonia and I often used it
to play *Hide-and-seek.* Her thumb would touch the screen
in on-off flashes to duck mine. For intimacy in our texts,
I began using emoticons. Texting is the most important
way to communicate in a long-distance relationship.
Besides telepathy of course, which we seem to share.
I lost count of the times I picked up the phone only to get
a notification from her. Juggling a career-in-the-making
and a long-distance relationship—our first—is intense
for anyone.

　　m(_ _)m, I pasted from Google.

***

I circled the rim of my coffee mug.

　　The *Tumblr* gremlin in me tapped the 't' icon. I
had followed several bloggers for lifestyle inspiration.
I tapped over to *Pinterest* and repinned a loft with an
exposed masonry. I had squirreled pictures, pinning my
dreams on the digital corkboard. I could see Sonia and
me canoodling against plush upholstery. Knocking back
swigs of specialty coffee, thumbing through back issues
of *KINFOLK.* Sonia once spotted a gleaming Airstream
trailer parked outside *Daikanyama T-Site.* Chin upon my
hand, I saw us stretching our legs next to one. Rustic and
homespun. Swilling brew under a gorgeous gloam before
sleeping under the stars. That, I am sure, is how heaven
looks like. I glanced again. The board revealed much of
my personality and made me more aware of my feelings.
And I was growing jealous. Jealous of people who get to
see Sonia every day.

　　I need to see her soon.

#LoveAtFirstLike #RealityBytes

Next > **Out of 6,972, 848, 504 people, we met.**

Out of 6,972, 848, 504 people, we met.
1 Oct 2011

I hate giving run-of-the-mills. There is no meaning. So I would buy little knick-knacks and put them together in a new way.

The Instagram logo had a rainbow so I got a music-box that chimed *Somewhere Over The Rainbow* and removed the mechanism. I designed a backing card with a smooching couple. After embellishing the tiny instrument with a puffy *Instagram* pin, I cranked one last time. Watching the teeth trip the metal comb, I wound it back to the start before putting it away. I made a second one. *Here for Sonia, here for me.*

Ta-da. Time for a well-deserved nap.

***

4:50.

Lanced by terror, I sprang to my feet and stumbled for a cab. The lights glowed brighter as I swerved to find the check-in counter. The rest of the world churned like a Van Gogh masterpiece. The counter was cordoned off with a red belt. It was a 5am flight.

"You're late."

I pinned a long look. The security guard whispered to the counter staff. She looked over and after forever, beckoned. I bolted across the airport to Gate 16 (I still keep the stub).

As the plane's tyres lifted from the tarmac, so did my heart. Relief suffused with the incandescence of the breaking dawn. I fixed a gaze at the vanishing orb, glad that I could make it in time. Leaning back in my seat, I stretched my legs to steady jangly nerves—only to recoil in a startle. I raised my phone to pretend toggling it to *Airplane mode.* And sneaked furtive glances at Morgan Freeman. Or a flight crew who looked like him. He flicked a look at a watch with a wooden band. Morgan Freeman with style to throw. I could not wait to tell Sonia later, skimming over the flight path.

I shimmied along the gangway after touchdown, peering over the misted panels. The air at Narita International Airport was thick in a tingle. I jostled for my passport, grinning as I thrust them at the customs officer. Slipping into the gents, I peered into the mirror, glancing right and left. *Not bad after a 7-hour flight,* I thought, smoothing the lapels. Scrunching my hair for more pouf, I fingered the fringe. Not bad at all, this new hair wax. Then I shoved my hands under the dryer to warm them.I swiped an imaginary lint off my new coat and stepped out, flicking a last look at the mirror.

As I tapped my boots against the trolley by the carousel, a mingling curdled. *What if we have nothing to talk about in real life? How will I manage with my Japlish?* We will see how. It is too late anyway, brushing aside the flurries. Hurrying down the escalator, I tossed a stubborn sling over my shoulder. I did not know what to do with my hands so I waved, straps and twerking heart. Like living in a music video.

"Sonia!"

And so we met—this time for real.

***

That night Sonia brought me to *Roppongi Hills*. We ducked under the giant spider sculpture, crunching red leaves and went up to the 52th floor of *Mori Tower*. To the tittering *Tokyo City View* observation deck. I panned, looking on the mass of twinkling lights. Jitters began slinking.

I had a feeling my life was going to change forever.

***

We pulled up at a rest stop en route to *Hakone* to grab—what else—coffee. Sonia and I came across an amazing vending machine. There is a video camera fixed inside so you can see coffee-brewing 'live'. All to the tink of *Coffee Rumba*. How the Japanese are sticklers for decorum is comforting. I am a sucker for routine. Mom had taught me to buy cake during my first day at school. I had the same thing for six months straight. What is wrong with sticking to the tried-and-tested? Nothing beats the prim.

At the inn, I gave Sonia the musical box. She cried. The mortified fling of the clock. The desperate flail for a cab. The mad frenzy at the airport.

Lo and behold, everything was worth it.

#lit #LoveWasJustAWordBeforeWeMet

Next >Tasty to nasty.

Tasty to nasty.
11 Oct 2011

As we alighted from the bus, I stole another glance at Sonia. I lugged a heart that grew heavier by the second. Good thing they do not charge excess baggage for that. As I dragged my feet, with a rippling sway, everything before me became a bokeh. I tried to blink it away but it got worse. I swiped my eyes with the back of my hands and hunted for PA speakers that would announce a one-day delay. We headed to the open-air observation deck, my footsteps echoing a final cadence. We want to breathe the same air for a little longer. As I stepped away from the officer, I turned for one last look at Sonia. There. Absolutely still. Trying hard not to bawl, just as I was.

I could not believe this. Anticipation ratcheted for months only to end in this. So many things had happened, but only one was on my mind.

When will I see Sonia again?

#NothingSweetAboutParting

Next > So close yet so far.

2

So close yet so far.
30 Dec 2011

1. Haji Lane
2. Marina Bay Sands SkyPark
3. Wicked Musical

I scrawled *Singapore Flyer* and struck it off. Then I wrote it down again. It would be Sonia's first visit to Singapore. Planning her itinerary split my head. Now I know how she felt before my visit. A meticulous planner, Sonia took care of the smallest detail. To live like a local, we would experience the speciality of the vicinity we were visiting. I am no planner. I just wanted us to explore alleys peddling hodgepodge. Binge-watch *SMAP X SMAP*. Head to art exhibitions. So long as *I* becomes *We*. After all the crossing out of days, it is a whirlwind of catching up. All the normal things couples do. Movies. Dinners. Shopping. When I was in Tokyo, I even joined Sonia's daily work commute. I remember twirling her slender fingers as we eyed the station staff while he shoved passengers. The frisson of seeing Sonia again after only eight hours was a sharp contrast to the bleary-eyed hordes. I gathered my thoughts and headed back to the tenderest headache ever.

While Sonia was in town, one of my wishes came true. I brought her to see Grandma. Grandma has dementia and lived in a nursing home. Sonia poised a hand. She took Grandma in a tender grasp, circling a thumb gently. Grandma could not speak but her withered hands told stories. Stories of how she patted me to sleep. Grandma turned to me, lips quivering as if something was going to surface. That something never did. She could not even remember her favorite grandson now. And I could never forget how she and Sonia held hands. Dementia takes away the person you remember. The grief is devastating. Looking away, I wished I would never lose another loved one to grief.

That did not come true.

#AbsenceDoesntMakeTheHeartGrowFonder

Next > **Bean in love.**

Bean in love.
08 Aug 2012

I jerked up for another peek. My favorite picture. I had
snapped it during my first Tokyo trip. A whimsical horse
photo-holder perched on Sonia's window sill, with rays
bursting through. The flare shimmered as dawn broke, slow
and even. Serenity. It got to be my favorite because of the
backstory. The picture was taken when I was with Sonia as
she rushed to work. I remember how Sonia munched her
nattō spread as I tried other angles. The pungent smell. The
sticky strings of slime. Yikes. I began imagining the pictures
that we are going to take at *Kamakura* the seaside town one
day. They are going to be glorious.

Back to work. Wading through, I saved more pictures
of skies in the folder. Sonia and I swapped a photo of the
sky every day. It would be our dating anniversary in less
than one week and I wanted to make a photo-mosaic
for us. Rolling black clouds. Sunshine peeping after the
storm. Incandescence cloaking the skyline. They are all
here. We live on different continents but we share the
same sky. 3000 miles apart but always together.

The glossy magazine. The song on *Spotify*. The Korean
TV drama. We share everyday experiences on the fly. Not
to boost a sense of security but to instill intimacy. As if
she were here. As if I were there. As if we were together.

But sharing photos would never be enough. Sonia
once sent a selfie where she was all drenched through after
she had dodged a typhoon. It was heartbreaking. While
we had become snap-happy, ironically, our *Instagram*
became downright sad. I tapped on it to see my last post.
It prompted for the password ... which I had forgotten. A
far cry from posting every single day, waiting with anxious
peers for Sonia's 'like'.

During the weekends, we potter at home. We became
homebodies because we wanted to be in each other's
company. Unlike other long-distance couples, we rarely
stand by *Skype*. We preferred to send voice messages on chat
apps. That way, we could hear each other all day long.

I toyed with the idea of surprising Sonia with a visit for our anniversary. But I have a feeling I would be the one in shock when the credit card bill arrives. In the end, I settled for an online florist. Pixels and bytes are a godsend for any long-distance relationship. Technology not only narrows down space with a finger on the mouse but makes a hefty resource for fun gift ideas. Trawling the net, from animated greeting to iPhone wallpaper. Luckily I can parlay my design flair into this relationship.

Praise the Lord.

***

My phone chimed. Sonia had dropped me a photo of the bouquet. It turned out to be prettier than the thumbnail. Red plume in an exquisite raffia weave. But that is not what I wanted to see.

I want to see Sonia.

***

With a gleeful scowl, a monkey jams its finger up the nose of a bulldog alongside. Not to be outsmarted, the pug, with a straight-on gaze, sneaks over for a lip-curling yank.

Best friends forever.

That declaration is emblazoned above the stooges in a cheeky font. It is a sticker we had bought in *Harajuku*. The shop is a kaleidoscope of wacky designs. Sonia and I had spent an hour rummaging through endless zany mascots. But this adorable label is a no-brainer. Not because it features our Chinese zodiac animal signs. It *is* us.

Over the last few years, pourover garnered cultdom in the *Slow Living* movement. Water is trickled down the grounds in measured amounts from a slim sprout. I dig this method because it unveils the nuances of coffee. The clean flavor of a pourover beats an espresso hands down. As bubbles rise, so does the thrill. There is something uplifting to hand-hewn coffee, turning brewing from routine to ritual. Like many couples, we dream of having our own cafe. A cafe where we hustle and bustle in pinstripe aprons. Honed from *YouTube*, I will take charge of brewing pourovers. I watch the ground coffee swell as I add hot water in precise twirls.

I get ready to stop when the drip slows to a dither. Pouring out a little from the carafe, I sip, letting it linger. I take another slurp, swishing it around. Perfect. What a tasty brew. Looking up, my gaze meets Sonia. We trade knowing looks over the fizz of the steam wand.

Over the 3,000 miles between us.

#CoupleGoals

Next > Time with you is me-time.

Time with you is me-time.
09 Jan 2013

Sonia and I closed our eyes and puckered for a peck.

Then we slurped with earth-shattering might. We went for our first cupping session. *Maruyama Coffee* is a specialty coffee trailblazer in Japan. They started in 1990 as a roaster/retailer. Now a hugely successful bidder at auctions, they offer highly-prized coffee to knowing caffeine junkies. They organize regular cupping sessions to let their beans speak for themselves. Coffee cupping is the practice of evaluating its aroma, acidity and aftertaste. Shorn of accolades on the packaging, cupping is an impartial assessment. You rub shoulders with other coffeeheads, turning you into a bona fide caffeine junkie. I had found someone to share my coffee and watch seasons change. A girl who is always saying what I wanted to tell her.

***

Third Wave Coffee Movement is the appreciation of coffee as an artisanal beverage. Gone are days when you bemoan the lack of good coffee in Tokyo to stave off caffeine pangs. Helmed by specialty coffee luminaries, the Third Wave Movement surged fast and furious. One coffeeshop became the first outside the U.S. to carry *Intelligentsia coffee. Intelligentsia Coffee* is one of the Big Three of Third Wave Coffee, making this shop a must-try.

We found it at the end of a side alley after weaving through the labyrinth. Peering through the windows, we halted. Behind the counter stood a barista with the steely gaze of an assassin. Lined with sculpture chairs and intricate pottery, the shop felt like it was owned by art connoisseurs. The 'cooler than thou' ambience of the place was daunting for newbies like us. My eyes darted across the menu. "Kenya—"

"—Karatina," finished Sonia.

The barista informed us that it had run out and apologized. He recommended *Kenya Kangocho* and other 'fruity' coffee. Impressed. He sized up my preference so quickly despite a language barrier. After settling for *Bolivia Anjilanaka* and Cappuccino, the barista surprised us with two cups of *Santuario Geisha Colombia* ice coffee. He apologized (again) though it was my fault for the mix-up. *Santuario Geisha Colombia* teased with a vivacious acidity and refreshing jasmine aroma. The complexity of berry-like flavors was a testament to its lineage. After all, Geisha is a rare, much-sought-after coffee varietal. *Bolivia Anjilanaka* jolted with its delectable juicy notes. Stone fruit and pear, finishing in nutty chocolate. Between sips, I approached the barista to get the spelling right for my taste notes. He offered a foil packaging; all the information I needed was on it.

It was almost closing time; the barista was busy rinsing a paper filter on the dripper. Rinsing with hot water gets rid of the papery taste and heats up the ceramic dripper. As we got up to return the cups, he spoke: "Do you have a bit of time?" He was in the midst of preparing complimentary cups of *Kenya Kangocho.* Sonia and I swapped looks of disbelief.

Flabbergasted by his generosity, I muttered my thanks. While savoring the full-bodied coffee, I was lost in thought. This is an age where interpersonal relationships have drifted apart. The barista's gesture is touching. Such incredible act of service is a testament to passion. Passionate people embrace work, friends and above all, life, wholeheartedly. Perhaps that is why they say coffee drinkers make better lovers.

A week later, we went back to buy beans for some DIY action. We stepped in to hale-and-hearty "Konnichiwa!" from Mr Barista and his lady colleague. He introduced new arrivals; we settled on *Amigos De Buesaco Colombia.* The lady packed our purchase into a paper carrier while Mr Barista preheated the dripper. This time he wanted to treat us cups of hot *Santuario Geisha Colombia* (we had it served cold the first time). We chatted as he coaxed flavors from the grounds, and received valuable tips.

Mr Barista kindly gave us spare paper filters without asking if we needed any. Again, we were impressed by his thoughtfulness. There was no attempt to up-sell other merchandize; service was delivered with pure empathy. As we got up to collect our purchase, Mr Barista gave us a brew guide for reference. He said the figures indicated had been changed and took the trouble to correct them for us.

As we rode the train back, Sonia laid the paper carrier on her lap. She peered in and shot bewilderment. There was something else.

A bag of *Zirikana Rwanda* beans.

Astonishment broke the silence as we realized what Mr Barista did. He had secretly slipped in another pack of beans as a gift. Left speechless by yet another act of wonderful service, my lips pursed to suppress the rush of ambivalence. Surprise. Gratitude. This is a unique trait of the Japanese culture. Japanese do not verbalize everything. They make an effort to understand others' feelings without asking outright. This is why most people are considerate in Japan. Sonia explained that Mr Barista's selfless act exemplifies *Omotenashi*. Loosely translated, it is an ancient philosophy of having 'selfless desire to put others first'. Mr Barista remains a beautiful memory of our Tokyo Coffee Trail. One that we look back fondly with gratitude and respect. Our Tokyo Coffee Trail is unforgettable, truly. The first time I drank my weight in coffee.

Live it up, drink it down!

#bae #OnFleek #HappinessIsACupOfCoffeeWithYou #WeShouldDoASingaporeCoffeeTrail

Next > **You are the tipple of my eye.**

3

You are the tipple of my eye.
30 Mar 2013

We are here for our much-awaited diving course.
    As we head to a clear blue bay, the burble of the jeep is dwindling my will protesting against after-lunch slump. We are on a gritty track hedged by thickets, verged by a grassy expanse. Wind-whipped waves tousle the sand with whitecaps that fade into nothingness. I can hear the guttural caws of seagulls. The sun bears down, hard, on my back as I twiddle with tubes. Sonia and I retreat to our parasols and I gulp the iced lemongrass tea. It trickles down and douses my parched throat. Flipping the beach towel, I lie down, turning to Sonia. I close my eyes and hold out my hand. Heaven, really.

A splutter of bangs in the sarcophagus-like MRI chamber woke me, if only for a while. Now you know how to wake a comatose person (I deserve a Nobel for this). Before I knew what was going on, I drifted to another dream.

The gnashing hiss of the rain is pierced by the ghoulish skyline. I am waiting out the pattering in a convenience store, flicking through magazines. I wonder if the flashes mean anything in morse code. Somehow, Sonia is not here. I wonder if this means anything too. I look out to the parking lot. It has started puddling. As if tears are falling from a rip in the sky onto the creases of earth. Deep rumbles tail— sometimes in a distant ripple, sometimes in a crash. Just then, I hear a trill. Silvery and singsong. Slicing through the din. I turn and see a lady at the payment counter, her back turned to me. Something is nagging. From the gentle nodding to the immaculate updo. It feels like a fortune cat beckoning me to the fire. And I am fighting the urge to go close. After a long moment, I turn back to the magazine in my hands. For some reason, it is shaking. But that is soon forgotten. The waft of fresh ink on paper is comforting and exciting all at once.

I wonder what will be on the next page.

#HeavenOnEarth

***

During the coma, I drifted to faraway lands. After five days, I veered back to consciousness.
     And reality.

Next > **Rise and whine.**

ACIDITY
The Hospital

4

Rise and whine.
03 Apr 2013

I woke up.

Drifted between two worlds. In, a blackness, out, the murky. Waking up from the coma is far from a flickering moment of being. A subtle awareness grew, heavy and laden. Something was wrong. Very wrong. I couldn't quite … yes. That must be it. Coffee. There was no coffee in the IV. I had always thought waking from a coma is like looking through the viewfinder of a camera as it focuses. A smear wavers until everything becomes crisp, locked in sight. But no, it wasn't. At least not for me. Instead my brain had strung together shreds of reality.

Just as well.

The two worlds became one again, but it will never be whole. Out for five days. I had collapsed during a football game, Brother said. 28 March. Good Friday night. A week after I turned 33. Shortly after the game began, the lads saw me falling over like a log. They scrambled over. My eyes had gone askew and I was gasping for air. They yelled my name. No reply. Then I stopped gasping. An off-duty fireman heard the *thwack* and ran over. He applied CPR while my friends called for an ambulance. Before the ambulance arrived, a biker medic came. I had no pulse so he whipped out the defibrillator. It only took two shocks to get my heart beating again. Turns out I can die another day. Not today. Not on Sonia's birthday.

Sonia.

Does she know? You bet. She had flown over. I had a cardiac arrest *and* a brainstem stroke. *My brain grew a stem? So much for vegging out.* A Pons stroke to be exact. A Pontine stroke to be more exact. The brainstem controls critical functions like heartbeat, breathing, eating and sleeping. To survive a brainstem stroke this well, you don't need a doctor. You need a miracle. I can't remember a thing about the incident. Which isn't a bad thing. Easier to remember nothing than forget everything. Sonia told me my first word out of coma is—wait for this—*Gmail.*

I wanted to swing a roundhouse kick at my … you get it. I know nothing of what she went through during the seven-hours flight. A red-eye flight, indeed. The desperate booking. The vigil over a comatose boyfriend. Watching the one who loves you sleep into dreamland is bliss. Watching the one you love sleep into nowhere is heartbreaking.

Addled by sedatives, life is a slur. The heart-stopping moment was caused by ventricular fibrillation (don't you just love medical jargons.) For those too lazy to click onto *Wikipedia*—a kind of cardiac arrest. The football game turned out to be too exciting for the faint of heart. And just like that, the rest of my life changed in one night.

To adversity, I say hello, hello, hello.

Mom said I had looked over my shoulder as I swung on the duffel bag, watching my nephew, Sebastian cackle before going off. Isn't it scary how every moment can be your last? *Now* can easily become *never*. And you will regret your only ever. There is no forever.

I couldn't see a damn thing now. I trotted out the glasses, fumbling. A grisly realization twisted.

Not the glasses. The eyes.

#shook

Next > **This is not a drill.**

This is not a drill.
06 Apr 2013

Nope.
Just, no. A big Hell No.
This can't be real.
The following weeks, an unreality wallowed. Does my head in to drive out my mind. Error 404. All I could come up was, "I shouldn't have gone for football that evening." I don't have hypertension, high cholesterol or diabetes. But why … why now? I am never given an answer. Life obviously doesn't take *know* for an answer.

Doctors' explanation left me little the wiser. How I got
a never-before-heard two-sided stroke is beyond hard
science. God, how can you let bad things happen to good
people? Wait a minute. are you even there?
This can't be real.
It can't be—
But so it is. I guess it's just one of those days.
Or months.
Or years, it would turn out.
For real.

***

I laid the urine bag on my lap. As a debutante-on-wheels,
I had no idea what to do with it. I slumped deep, hoping
I would sink into nothingness. Surely this can't be real. I
held out a hand and gave it a look-over. I couldn't quite
make out the fingers. Maybe, possibly, this didn't happen.
Maybe.
Maybe I had dozed off at a meeting. It had all been
another dream—a horrendous nightmare—and, pronto,
I would wake to find life as it was before.
I never did.
Definitely not maybe. Everything I can't imagine, is
real. I can't even.

***

Die. Die. Die. Everything that was born must die. It's
only a question of when. Thing is, we don't know how
long we have left to live—or die. So I already thought
of my epigraph: *Nothing is written in stone. See you soon.*
Fortunately—or unfortunately, you might say—my time is
not up yet.
An acid test awaited. Had to relearn everyday basics.
Walking. Talking. Of all things, I need to learn how to
unlearn everything I know. And we are only getting started.
Hell hath no fury like Life scorned.

#OhHelloThereAdversity #EyeCantBelieveThis

Next > **I see what you did there.**

I see what you did there.
09 Apr 2013

"Can you lift your buttocks", asked the voice, gentle
and lilting. As I did, I took a whiff, sifting through the
sickening deadness above and around me.

Jasmine. Fresh and sweet. Warm and friendly.
I might not see people but I could match their voices
and perfumes and silhouettes. My mind stopped riffling.
A-ha. It's the nurse with a foreign accent. The crispness of
the scent told me her shift had just begun. I'm all ears—
and nose—for the next couple of weeks. My eyes were
still askew, they told me. I could only make out people
from their voices and perfumes. With heightened senses,
I began to make sense of the senseless. "Now can you
turn over?" Lying on my side, I heard her face soften
into a smile.

My balance was so shot, I could not even sit upright
on my own. "The bed is tilted", I had whined to Dad. I'm
always woozy. Like in a perpetual hangover. My friend
remarked that I get to scrimp on the booze. But coffee is
my guiltiest guilty pleasure—especially African beans.
A crackerjack of aroma, acidity and aftertaste.

A dose of awesome.

#SeeTheSmell

Next > **Not all that takes your breath away is epic.**

5

Not all that takes your breath away is epic.
12 Apr 2013

When you can't see shit, you can't do shit. It is hard to eat when you can't see. Actually, everything is hard—believe me—awfully hard, when you can't see.

And I can see why.

Life. Sometimes the only way out is beastmode. I will try my damnedest to plough (and plough) through the shit that is life.

Not that there is much of a choice. When you are down to nothing, how you face anything is everything. I can't give that up. Not yet. Yes. Bliss suffers from ADHD. And yes, I had a stroke for no reason. But no, I'm not going to give up. There's much to be done. It might be daunting. But I will, I will. And I closed my eyes.

Ah yes … hello darkness, my old friend.

***

Woo boy.

Breathing is hard. Unbelievably hard. It had never occurred to me just how breathing could be so hard. The doctors had planned to wean me off the ventilator. They had given me an emergency procedure in ICU. A hole was cut through the front of my throat and into my windpipe to hook me to a ventilator. I had always thought of breathing as God-given. A matter of course. But breathing is still not the hardest damn thing.

Drinking water is.

***

It was feeding time. Because I couldn't swallow, I had to be fed through a tube. There was a sombre hum as the nurse raised the bed. I held back an urge to claw out as she filled the tube. Coldness festered. As the sludge fell down my nostril, a choking despair rose. I had not felt so desperate in a long time—never ever—and began flailing. They tied me with restrainers to curb more outbursts.

***

We had queued for Tempura Donburi for two hours once, Sonia and I. The throng nosed through the alley. To kill time, I decided to do a real-time translation of the two lads in front. One tapped three fingers on his left palm. So that's how divvying up one salary turned into three servings of tofu. And ever since, it became our very own three-finger salute, a secret hand sign for my favorite food.

Farther up, there was an old man in a cream-coloured sweater. Done with my 'live' commentary, I budged from one foot to the other and watched him. Hunched over a cane, he shuffled along, sometimes giving a low cough. As Sonia and I walked away, smacking our lips, I wondered. I don't understand the old man. Why will anyone want to go to such length for food?

Now I know why. It's the little things that make life great. They remind you what it means to be alive.

***

She propped an arm, her white coat brushing the bed rail. I caught a soothing whiff. Homely. "This may be a little uncomfortable", she said, as a penlight darted from one eye to the other. "How are you today?" The doctor clicked off.

"Dizzy"

"On a scale of one to ten, how will you rate it?"

"Eight."

And that was that. I was furious. What's the point of asking if you do nothing.

"When will I be okay?"

"In no time."

It was gone before it was there. But I saw it. A fleeting unknowingness.

I *saw.*

***

The next morning, I scoured the head-rush, long and hard, for any come-hither signals. *Wrong man, witch-hunters.* I winced and realized I could see if I closed one eye. And with that, days as *Jack Sparrow* of the Rehabilitation Ward began. I could text Sonia again. She flew back the day I woke. These days, she gets anxious when she receives radio silence.

I could only imagine the jitters writhing around her throat before breaking into an iron grip. All while she wrangled over the *everything-is-fine* mask. I could only imagine Sonia stepping into the apartment, shedding her mask at the foyer. Not for long, though. At the rate I'm going MIA, the mask would soon be creased onto her for good. With it, she could pass off going about everyday life when in fact, everyday life is going about her. But that wasn't the only thing she had to pretend. We still chatted every day. Or tried to. It wasn't until I hit *replay* that I knew how badly I slurred. Even I couldn't make out the watery drawl. I had to listen again and again to claw back sense. She must have pretended to understand. I wonder how the mask would look on her.

Slumped here, I could only imagine.

#EatToLive #LiveToEat

Next > The grasp of wrath.

The grasp of wrath.
22 Apr 2013

The word is out.
Why. Not even *why me.* Just *why.*
And why not?
—*Why Do You Do What You Did?*

I seriously question the wisdom of questioning. I asked Dad many questions. *Why* beamed a noun, adjective and a verb that seared. On second thought, it's a silly question. Wouldn't have been me if Dad could answer it. 'Why?' I brayed. "What have I done to rile this mighty wrath?"

Wouldn't I like to know.

Even doctors are stumped, let alone the wider world. Nothing presaged such a devastating illness. The stroke is unthinkable. Beyond belief. How I had a stroke at 33 remains an absurdity, making it something straight from BuzzFeed WTF. But sometimes there is no why. Too much navel-gazing is pointless. Those who know, know. Those who don't, stop searching. There might never be an answer. I looked heavenward, glassy and distant, but saw only dingy ceiling panels. I laid my glasses on the nightstand and had time for a last thought before my eyes fell close.

I hope this isn't my only one nightstand.

#EyeCantBelieveThis

Next > **When a therapist becomes the rapist.**

When a therapist becomes the rapist.
24 Apr 2013

Lucky? Duh. I shoved my shins. Spasms made it hard to put my feet on the footrests. I had felt a thump as I wheeled to the gym. I looked over my shoulder and glanced right up at the doctor. Then, I grabbed the hand-rims and lurched along the hallway for some wind-in-the-face cruising. *Must be some really wild luck.*

A compensatory strategy for breath control (or lack thereof) is pausing and phrasing. You break up words into smaller chunks. And that is how 'therapist' becomes 'the rapist'. Every therapy session is a mind rape, leaving me crestfallen time and again. Humble pie is dessert of the day. For the life of me, I can't even budge my foot anymore.

Next up is crawling. Yes, you heard right. I had to learn crawling. Crawling is a lot of hand-eye coordination, balance—and anguish. When a baby starts crawling, it's adorable. Me? You gotta be kidding! My ego was further pummelled when I couldn't get it right. I got down on my hands and knees again and skimmed over the crawlspace. It felt odd, simply odd, like something had gone a little off. A lot off, actually. Horribly awry. Something is missing. Then the wrongness hit me, all in one go … the ring and flowers.

It is hard to put your best foot forward when earth's natural forces seem to be acting strange. As if gravity is pushing up the balls of my feet, confirming what I already know: my world has turned upside down. A lot of my exercises are for core strengthening. Obviously, the therapists knew their shit. You need a steely core for a battle without nemesis. Sadly, no one ever wins in a war.

Between sit-ups, I watched an amputee struggle to balance between the parallel bars. Amputees need flexible limbs so that prostheses fit well. Physical therapy helps by "waking up" residual limbs soon after surgery. He hesitated. Then he stood up, doubtfully—a little fearfully—tottered and fell back to the wheelchair. I heaved in a slow gasp and turned my gaze to my knees. Some loss can be forever. It's a good thing I didn't lose my mind. Occupational therapy after a stroke involves coping with disabilities and relearning everyday tasks. The hospital has an ADL corner. A one-room apartment mockup where you practise activities in a home-like setting. After the fluorescent tube flickered, I looked around. The pain of living. Eating. Bathing. Cleaning. Agony of Damned Living.

Sometimes, the therapist would take me out for community walks. I caught passers-by gawking. I could feel the glares. The worse is when they turn their heads to continue eyeballing. As if they can't get enough. As if being lampooned by life is not enough. At first, I felt like the star of a circus show. The chaperoning therapist a ringmaster. But that's my own reading, I realized. So I switched tack. According to the laws of aerodynamics, bees can't fly. They do anyway because they don't give a shit to what others think. Since I couldn't change the way others look at me, I tipped my own perspective. I just take it that the prying eyes are staring at my tattoo and not let this bother me … too much.

In the other news, my life changed (again).
I had learned to swallow.

***

"Anyone can use that," I muttered as my eyes pulled away. The therapist was about to teach me how to use a frame walker. You stand between the frame, lift both ends together and place it ahead.

She paused for one moment and said,

"Try using one arm."

"How," I said, shaking my head.

"I … can't."

"But you just said anyone can."

My breath fell away in a rush. I sucked in and got up from the wheelchair. Stop taking things for granted. The things you are granted can be taken. Same goes for people. Especially the one whom you think will always be there.

You.

***

Stirring coffee and washing hands. The simplest things in life are hardest to learn. Things I never imagine I have to learn. The stroke had wiped out my fine motor skills. My hands could no longer perform precise movements. Like stirring coffee. I would reach for the spoon and grasp in a twitchy clutch. That's all. Unleashing all my Force, I simply couldn't make the soft twirl.

Time for the trump card. A normal swirl would produce a vigorous spin, agitating coffee brew long after stirring stops. A more precise technique gleaned from my cupping sessions is to stir in a cross motion. Like drawing a '+' with the spoon. It worked. I could stir coffee again.

In the hospital, washing your hands is a staid affair. There are seven steps for a thorough rub-down but I couldn't follow any of it. I could no longer scrunch and rub my hands when washing them. Only two steps for me:

1. Nudge on the soap dispenser.
2. Turn on the tap and hover my hand.

If only the stream would bear away my misery or dilute it—for a while at least.

***

The therapist wheeled me to a table with neat stacks of pegs. *More exercises for my hands,* I thought.

She handed over a deck of cards and left. *Peter Piper picked a peck of pickled peppers. She sells sea shells.* Tongue twisters. Spoken wordplay makes a great exercise for articulation, improving slurring. It strengthens and stretches speech muscles.

"Pe … ter—"

"—Peter …"

Maybe I needed a warm-up. I scrabbled at the card, nearly spilling the whole deck and started the next. I tried reading slower.

"S … S … She—", I mauled the word, gasping for another breath. I couldn't even get past the first word. I looked up. No one around.

For the first time after the stroke, I cried.

***

One time, after breakfast, the therapist wheeled me to a small table. It had vertical posts and rings in bubblegum shades, the kind you would find in a Fisher Price playpen.

"Can you sort them by color?" I did. "Now can you stack them by size?" I did too. "Very good!" Then to my … bewilderment she commended with a pat. 2013 has been a year of many firsts. The first time I had surgery. The first time I used a wheelchair. The first time I felt like a circus seal.

And I have a feeling they would not be the last.

***

Some crumbs refused to budge as I struggled to sweep them off. Friends plied a stash of munchies, putting 'comfort' in 'food'. Coffee. Chocolate. Cookies. It felt so good, I feel bad. Other patients can't even swallow and here I am, munching away.

I wiggled to dump a wrapper, gripping the guard rail on the bed. It reminded me of the vertical grilles fencing my grandparents' balcony. Sitting beside my grandfather, I would dangle my legs through the grilles and swing my feet. The exhilaration of hanging your feet off the ground. Those were the days with nary a care in the world. But this is not a time to fawn over tender memories. There's much to be done.

Too much, perhaps.

***

"Can you clap?"

I looked at the therapist sharply. *This is ridiculous.* Then I held out my hands. No matter how hard I will them, they won't meet. I turned my palms over in disbelief. Stung. It takes more than two hands to clap. Clapping requires hand-eye coordination. I can't even clap now.

And this is most ridiculous.

#trolls #NoChildsPlay

Next > Going under the knife.

6

Going under the knife.
03 May 2013

Doctors are worried. Another Victoria's Secret Fashion Show just may give me another heart-stopping moment. They want to implant a defibrillator. If I get another cardiac arrest, it will shock my heart back into action (hopefully). Before that, they need to see if there's any blockage. They will thread a thin scope through a blood vessel in my thigh to see if there's any plague in need of clearing. Light fixtures flashed by as they wheeled me to the operating theater. Like familiar strangers you chance by in this frazzling babel.

"Can you tell me your name and I.D?" A man in neatly pressed scrubs asked, his voice oddly sharp through the mask.

Geneva Conventions?

Then a familiar darkness swept over, swift and forced.

After the surgery, doctors ordered a CRIB—wonderfully apt it would soon turn out—Complete Rest In Bed. Mom had to spoon noodles into my mouth. It dribbled all over my chin despite her best efforts.

Mom spoon-fed me when I was a kid. Now she has to do it again. Life is fair but not square. It has gone full circle like a revolving door. I can't understand why I had a stroke at 33. It is one of the riddlesome mysteries of Life, one I could never—ever—unfurl.

#BoobJob

Next > **Life, however grave, can't stop a crave.**

Life, however grave, can't stop a crave.
05 May 2013

ICU. High-dependency Ward. And now, Standard Ward. I switched wards quicker than Hugh Hefner changed Playgirls.

The old man in the opposite bed groused. He was admitted for a clogged heart and had not smoked for a day. A man in the adjacent bed snapped up, cussing good old politics. The burly young chap on the left groaned, scabrous-voiced. He had broken his ribs when his motorcycle skidded.

I tuned to politics for a while. The debate was soon disrupted like someone nudged the radio knob. Old man with the clogged heart had shuffled out. He came back with a wheelchair. The young chap, amid heavy whimpers, gingerly lowered the bed rail. He edged his legs over and hesitated. But nothing could stop him. On a drawn breath, he clambered onto the wheelchair. His face pinned a grimace. The old man must know telepathy. That chap could barely speak. Old man with the clogged heart wheeled him past an empty nurse station (such meticulous planning), heading to the toilet for a fag. I feel them.

Cigarettes and coffee. I have the same craving for coffee. Not just any old coffee. Specialty coffee.

May the Lord save me

#Unstoppable

Next > **Cross my heart and hard to die.**

Cross my heart and hard to die.
10 May 2013

Nuzzling the angry puff with my chin, I looked down at the implant scar. The tip of my nose got in the way. I felt like a puppy chasing its own tail. As my fingertip traced the edges, I remember what my therapist said. She had joked that my heart implant could trigger the supermarket alarm. I had looked at her and replied with a smile, a little tiredly. Now I will—eat this, Bruce Willis—Die Hard With A Defibrillator.

And I couldn't help but marvel at technology. Even a heart surgery needs no stitches. Physical wounds heal first. Other wounds take time.

But when?

#ManBoob

Next > **There is no better time than yesterday.**

7

There is no better time than yesterday.
21 May 2013

The nurse slathered deftly, avoiding the wound. When she approached my calf, there was a moment of silence. As if the thought of watering the vintage roses came to her.

"Were you very naughty?" she asked as she continued scrubbing with the baby head-to-toe shower wash (the same that Sebastian uses. I wonder how The Precocious One is doing now. Teacher had rung Mom to bring his Blanky down during his first day at school.) Her strange question caught me. Then it struck me. My leg tattoo had snared her curiosity. Tattoos carried a hefty stigma. But I regret nothing. Okay, except maybe regret. Because regret is forever. I don't want to lie in an old-age home, kept awake by should-haves. Vintage floral motifs and cascading waves covered half my right calf. I remembered my mum's reaction. "That big?" she said, wide-eyed.

"Big? It's still unfinished".

Like my life now, many things are left undone. Lying on the bed, I drew up a bucket list on my phone. All simple items. No bungee jumping or Northern Lights or travel round the world. It turned out to be more like a to-do list. I hit the trash can icon. You don't start compiling a bucket list when you nearly kick the bucket. A sense of remorse swelled, quickening, as I remembered how I frittered my time. I had always wanted to bring my family on an overseas vacation. But I thought it would be better when Sebastian gets older. Silly me. There's no such thing as the best time.

It's the only time. The *only*. I lay against an arm slung over the pillow, reproachful. And—only now—rued the many yesterdays I said tomorrow.

If not now, when?

#ICould #IWould #IShould #InTheEnd #IDidnt

Next > **It's a bird … It's a plane …
It's a bolt out of the blue.**

It's a bird … It's a plane … It's a bolt out of the blue.
04 Jun 2013

Superman.

That's what doctors call me. Brainstem stroke patients rarely survive so well. But my days are angst-ridden, festered by the lament that no tPA was given. (tPA is a clot-busting drug administered within three hours of symptoms onset for strokes.)

People say that when things are falling apart, they are actually falling in place. They better be. They seem to be hailing all over like an upturned snow globe. A friend said that I had used up a lifetime of good karma. Any grouse would be churlish. How lucky to not end up in a folder on the coroner's desk. So, yeah, I'm grateful for surviving but I am miserable being caged by my disabilities. This morning, I squirmed after just nine push-ups and nearly gave up. *Snap out of it,* I waggled under my breath, *be thankful you aren't lying in bed.* Severe brainstem strokes can cause the locked-in syndrome. A condition in which survivors can move merely their eyes. Clenching deep, I shoved the ground. With a judder, the implant wound without stitches burst into a mist of ooze and the rest of me expunge into nothingness.

Or so I wished.

Like the cartoon I remember from *MAD* magazine. A zit-riddled lad stands at a mirror, whistling away. Crooking two fingers, he pops one. Thick pus hits the mirror in a splodge. He watches in growing horror as it erupts into a gush. His innards spew all over until nothing of him is left. If only that can happen now. If only nothing of this nightmare is left.

If only.

#ManOfSteel #HeartOfFeel

Next > Yes, I mean no.

Yes, I mean no.
28 Jun 2013

Sometimes *yes* really means *no*. Life is not always a clear black-and-white. Sometimes you have to look in the darkest white. I told Mom and Dad not to stay till visiting hours are over. But when they went away, so did my sanity. I couldn't put a finger on this feeling. Never had it before. I laid my palms over my tummy and watched the whirring ceiling fan. Then, realization hit.

I'm homesick. This is, after all, the first time I'm away from home.

One morning, an elderly patient died. The nurse was nonchalant, humming a tune as she doled out breakfast. The same nurse who sang to him. The same nurse who would sit him in a wheelchair, buckling his safety belt before giving him a shave. The same nurse who bantered with him as she filled his feeding tube.

All as he lay unconscious.

The duty doctor had called his family down for last goodbyes. They began sobbing by him as the nurses swished the drapes. A man fumbled them and stepped out. He swerved partway from the bed, whipping off his glasses and swiped his head on the crook of a sleeve. Jabbing it back, he hastily stepped back. Moments later, the sobs screeched into wails. I looked away. What a beautiful morning. A washed-out amber had swept over.

It's not the end of the world. It only feels like one.

Laying back, I shut my eyes and stared into the abyss. A slavering blackness. I thought of when I could walk. Of when I could talk.

Of when *yes* means *yes*.

***

After four months of "Yes, I mean, no", it's time to ditch the ill-fitting garb.

#YouCanAlwaysMakeMoney
#YouCantAlwaysMakeMemories

Next > Changes + more changes. Life = Struggle.

AFTERTASTE
Life After Stroke

8

Changes + more changes. Life = Struggle.
17 Jul 2013

Yes. I mean, no.

You can't fight a stroke. But you can live with it. Cheek by jowl. Yes, I can still make coffee. No, not with my old rig. I celebrated my homecoming with leftover specialty coffee beans. The hand grinder sat on the shelf, godforsaken, next to the *Montblanc* pen Sonia gave me. Placing a clasp over the grip, I turned. Or tried to. It refused to budge. *I can do this,* I told myself, not at all sure. I tried again, grazing my knuckles with each jerk. Finally putting away the grinder and AeroPress in a small bucket, I hung it on the walker.

This is the first time I'm having specialty coffee since forever. *Achievement unlocked.* And besides, the coffeehead in me is dying to know how stale beans taste. For the first time in my life, coffee tasted just like how it smelled—dry and musty—as if the paper bag has melted into the beans.

But boy, does it feel good!

***

The AeroPress is a pièce de résistance for any bona fide caffeine junkie. It is a gadget with two cylinders, used for brewing coffee. It works like a syringe where steeped coffee is forced through a filter by pressing down one cylinder. With my retarded motor skills, making a pourover is impossible. AeroPress is a foolproof way to brew coffee. Okay, almost. Instead of measuring the water temperature, I used it straight from the dispenser. And I slopped coffee all over the counter. As Dad whisked my mug to the coffee table, I washed up. My knuckles stung from all the grinding. But all is worth it. This act of domestic violence in the name of coffee is absolutely necessary.

Life–if it can be called that–is amok with struggles. It clamored for change. New ways to live an old life. For starters, I had to bathe sitting down. Changing clothes too. Using an electric shaver (the safety razor is no longer safe). Making coffee is only possible with the AeroPress. I have to retire my pourover dripper till God-only-knows-when. But some things won't ever change. I want Sonia to be happy then and now.

And perhaps, for the rest of forever.

#HomeIsWhereTheCoffeeIs

Next > **There's no feeling like home.**

There's no feeling like home.
20 Jul 2013

Every nook of my room bears tacit vignettes. Roiling memories of a distant past. I skimmed away at the white shelf. A music box. A Tokyo city guide. A—

I flinched.

—sketchbook. I was supposed to compile a scrapbook for our Tokyo Coffee Trail. And call it *CREMA SUTRA*. Late-night TV meant it never happen. I remember how Sonia and I cavorted along the aisles of *Dean & Deluca*. Blissfully clueless that things would soon go south—not the south I would have enjoyed. So let me save you some time. It doesn't pay to postpone life because time runs out. Time is free. But it's also priceless. You can't have more—you *make* it.

What are you waiting for?

***

My existence had been stripped away, all at once, to a single cabinet at the hospital. My wardrobe staples had become unfamiliar. With sartorial cues culled from Tumblr and Pinterest, I remember decking out in ankle-baring pants and polka dot polo tees.

Peeking into the wardrobe, I saw punchy clothes neatly stacked. Like love letters you find only after breaking up. Atop one stack laid a chambray shirt from Sonia. I could not bring myself to wear it as I felt it was way too expensive.

Now I wonder what would happen to it if I had died.

#HomeSweetHome

Next > **Smash or pass.**

Smash or pass.
05 Aug 2013

An adversity is an usurper of contentment. One that butchered me to a pulp with a lightning bolt. It lurks in shapeshifting forms. For some, it may be a relationship or career. For me, it's health. A hideously vengeful one. One that masqueraded as bliss and slunk away in a wait to tug the carpet.

If there's anything worth fighting, this is it. It's my life after all. Never argue with fate. Fight it. Fight it all the more. If I don't, who would? One day we will all succumb to death. Until then, never succumb to life. Life is to be lived.

At any rate, the stroke didn't kill me. It's just another kick-in-the-face adversity that scuppered my life. Every now and again, adversity creeps out of its lair and shakes life with a devastating payload. But it's not the end. It's just an intervention. I would have chosen a more genteel adversity. Not this *Attila the Hun*. But then, you don't get to choose the kind of setback which rocks your world. How you face it, though, is entirely your own pick. I might be destined for a life of sex, drugs and rock 'n' roll. If this is life's idea of *rock*, I can't imagine what's *roll*. Just bring on the sex and drugs.

I wanna go out with a bang, thank you very much.

#ItTakesDarknessToSeeStars

Next > **The boy who fangirls over beans.**

9

The boy who fangirls over beans.
08 Dec 2013

Coffee. Because coffee. Who cares why.

It's a two-thumbs-up *Ethiopia Heirloom* this morning. Making coffee after you wake is different from preparing one in the afternoon. Lovely, as always. I'm a morning person only because of coffee.

With each crank, I counted my blessings. What a grateful moment, partaking in the poetics of a daily routine. More than a brekkie pick-me-up, it's a ritual not a routine. Circling the rim of my mug, I watched the wisps. Cathartic. I raised the mug to my lips, thudding my teeth, sloshing the coffee. I sipped and swirled it in my mouth before sliding down the rocket fuel. Before long, I tossed back the last relish, ready to take on a spanking new day. Life should be killin' it.

Not killin' me.

***

You should be able to deal with all obstacles, as long as you ask for help when needed. So says my horoscope.

Say what? As I squared the newspapers, I flicked a glance at the front page. I sat up. Singapore's first riot in forty-five years. Skimming over, I mulled over what wasn't reported.

More days of tumult ahead.

***

I edged the newspaper higher to duck her. Not that I could hide anything from Mom. The therapist had asked me to consider an electric wheelchair. "So what's your decision?" Mom lifted her eyebrows, taking me in a wary gaze.

I shook my head and realized she couldn't see it. "I hadn't decided yet." Maybe I should discuss with Sonia too. So I did and Sonia fell silent. Silence is an answer too.

Just not the one I want to hear.

#TheAnswer

Next > Mom knows best. Dad, the rest.

Mom knows best. Dad, the rest.
11 Jan 2014

I don't need 140 characters. Only one word sums up my life
now. Mum's the word. Or Dad for the matter.

Mom dyes her hair every month. When did she grow
so old? I skirted my glance across a white patch, sipping
my long-cold coffee. How *old* is she now. And our overseas
holiday … Never ever let someday be one day when it
could have been yesterday. It's not the things we do that we
regret. It's the things we don't. I had been too busy with
life, jettisoning Mom and Dad. I didn't pay attention to
Mom and Dad nearly enough. I wonder now how many
times she has to dye her hair before I can stand on my own
again. Getting back to work. And soon. Time is snapping
at my heels. Mom and Dad are not getting any younger.
We are, so very often, too busy growing up to realize our
parents growing old. I had been completely—overly, now it
seems—engrossed. Once, Dad held the passenger door for
me, and it was then, I noticed how grizzled he had become.
Mom and Dad, I won't have a stroke again when I'm 33.

I promise.

***

It feels strange when Dad pushes me to my acupuncture
sessions. I am now dependent on who should have been
my dependents. To pinch pennies I sleep with no air-
conditioning these days. Shit had hit the fan but I had
to switch it on. That's the only way I could save on the
electricity bill. Jobless, I contribute only carbon dioxide to
the household. The irony of life sliced like a papercut on my
tongue as Dad wheeled me. 30 years ago, the man behind
pushed my pram. And now he's pushing my wheelchair.

The physician swiped firmly, as if to mark the spot like
a tattoo artist. Then with a sleight of hand, she thrust. As
she poked the rest, I feel like a voodoo doll at the mercy
of an overzealous shaman. She had suggested needling the
tongue. But I protested. Just ink, no kink, please. Body

piercing is out. I grimaced as she pierced the edge of the palm, wishing I'm a peasant with laser-resistant callus.

But nothing was as unbearable as the ordeal upon me.

***

Sometimes I wish for a swashbuckling ally who could haul me out of this wormhole. I would seize the chance to scuttle.

I wish.

#IBelieve #ButWheresTheMagic

Next > **The pain of living in vain**

The pain of living in vain.
21 Feb 2014

A throb ached through my jaw. I swallowed a couple of painkillers, hoping it will go away by morning. I had hundreds of them left over from my hospital stay. I wasn't in pain—not the physical kind anyway—so I didn't take any. Besides, painkillers don't kill pain. They are in cahoots, in fact. Pain circles in a fearsome lurk behind, waiting to pounce. And when they do, they strike with a vengeance.

Heartless. No chance at all. And, true enough, they did so the next morning. The dull throb became an ice pick.

"Is it going to hurt?" I wondered aloud to the dentist as I shoved the other leg over the reclining seat.

"It won't. Especially for you," he replied, eyes flicking over my tattoo. "It'll be over before you know it." My tattoo is misleading. People think I fight pain well. No, you can't fight it. Especially the pain of living.

#NoPainkillerForLife

Next > **Young in years. Old at heart.**

10

Young in years. Old at heart.
05 Mar 2014

Neurology. Cardiology. Endocrinology. Ophthalmology.
Follow-up appointments reveal glimpses of human frailty.
The physicality of aging. As we grow old, our bodies
become decrepit shells. I jumped the gun and arrived at the
party too early.

As I watched people wheeling elderly parents, I
remember what Sonia and I saw in Yokohama. There
was a skating rink outside the Red Brick Warehouse. A
throng had burgeoned. I peered over the heads to catch
a brilliance of yellow. A man in his 70s clad in bright ski
pants. He spun in dizzying swirls before swerving in a
spray of grit. The swagger of a man who knew that the
world is at his feet. I'm only half his age and here I am.
I propped myself up as the man who barely stayed alive
thought about the man who stayed young. After a while I
hoisted myself.

Dad had stepped out of the pharmacy.

#MyFountainOfYouthBroke

Next > **That which I … I don't know.**

That which I … I don't know.
15 Mar 2014

Sonia leaned her head while listening during one of our
Skypes. This wretched what-if could sever our lives. But I
could not expect Sonia to plough through this brutality.
To take up arms and face this fall-out alongside. That
would be too selfish. As much as it hurts to think about,
I'm all too aware that she needn't go through this. She has
given her best. My words were careful, deliberately slow.

"Life—" I trailed off, "—wants what it wants."

So after, she said: "What do *you* want?" Sonia nudged, gently but firmly, with a soft tip.

"I just—"

She smiled.

"—I just want you to be happy."

She smiled again.

And with that, our discussion ended. No need to broach other plans. I don't have the faintest idea what comes after.

Three days later, the postman rang. Coffee beans from Tokyo.

#IDontWantLife #IWantHappy

Next > Being thankful for what I have.

Being thankful for what I have.
18 Mar 2014

I yowled.

A sharp pain split my lip. I had bitten myself again. My mouth felt swollen with numbness after the stroke, which makes eating hard. Like chewing with a cotton wedge. My tongue curled forth and licked the coppery tang. Taste. It didn't exist during tube feeding. So thankful to be taken off. I'm more than happy to bite my lip and not the dust. Every morning, I would glide my tongue over crusted lips. Skirting around the sores, before reaching for my day-by-day pillbox. As I flipped the lid, I could feel time slipping by like a tear-away calendar. Before the stroke, I thought I had all the time in the world.

Indeed, I do. It is just not in my hands.

#StopComplaining #StartThanking

Next > When reality hits.

When reality hits.
19 Mar 2014

Things have gotten out of hand.

People would have thought one could dawdle a wee bit when recuperating. Anything but. I near enough have to rest in peace. Now I have to find rest in pieces. Nothing restful about being in pieces. I had to learn to eat and drink and pee and shit and walk and talk. Daily life is now chock-a-block with physical therapy, acupuncture and follow-up appointments. A far cry from a free-spirited former lifestyle. I was your everyday normal dude (okay maybe a little abnormal) until this hit.

Kids learn a great deal of motor skills. What I had learnt, when I was little, was completely gone. Not even capable of small tasks now. I had to work my ass off, relearning little things that nobody remembered learning. I'm grateful to start from Ground Zero. Utterly frustrating though, having to learn basic tasks all over again at the ripe old age of 34. You would think three decades of muscle memory makes it easier, but hell, no. The loss of dexterity made them fiendishly hard, if not outright 'impossibru'. And so the grilling begins.

Woot.

#GoMe

Next > **Happy re-birth day to me.**

Happy re-birth day to me.
21 Mar 2014

I looked on as the flame pranced.

Most people deem success by one measure—career. I'm approaching middle age and had nothing to show for it. Except for this life-toaster. One that flipped me the bird. No "Ready or not, here I come," as life segregated with B.C and A.D—*Before Crisis* and *After Disability*. What a twerp.

I heaved, happy to be 34 years old and not 33 years dead.

#NotGettingOld #GettingBetter

Next > Lost In Damnation.

Lost In Damnation.
26 Mar 2014

The iMac chimed as it booted up. I snooped through forgotten files and watched a video. Pain jabbed as I hit *Play*. The last of us before the stroke. I remember basking in pomp a la *Lost In Translation* at the Shibuya crosswalk. I watched it over and over as if something would change.

As if silence itself has become too heavy to bear.

A frame cut to a snow-dusted car park. One night it had begun snowing. It was the first time I saw snow. "It seldom snows in Tokyo. You're lucky," Sonia had said. I stood by the window, lulled by the flecks of blissfulness. They drifted, chorale-like in the wind, only to disappear on my cupped palms.

I felt a twinge over a tracking shot of our brewing paraphernalia. A parting shot of my last Tokyo sojourn. What was once saccharine now stalked a sense of loss and everything I couldn't be. And maybe, what would never be.

I clicked on an episode of *SMAP x SMAP.*

#SomeoneUpTherePressedPause

Next > Together we make my world.

12

Together we make my world.
19 Apr 2014

Adversity—a weapon of mass heartbreak. Particularly a crippling illness. Tormented as I am, never once did I throw a fit. Any outcry is futile. No amount of Gordon Ramsey fist-banging is going to change anything. I couldn't expect my family to pander to my whims. The thankless task of caregiving is draining enough. Caregivers need care too. I wanted to make their lives easier. At the very least, make myself less of a nuisance. The stroke is a battle with this whole other beast. But if anyone can pull off a survival, it's me. Of the many things I'm grateful for, none more grateful than the love I got. I realized now, there are so many people who loved me but never told me. People who made my world—or what was left of it—a better place. Grateful that fate was benevolent and didn't go straight for the jugular. Maybe it did, but missed. The head is pretty close. Whatever it was, I was glad that I survived in one piece. My life, however, was in a shambles. And I could not have picked a family I would want to be in more.

One that held up while I held out at the edge.

#Fam

Next > **Life. When adversity happens and shit never ends.**

Life. When adversity happens and shit never ends.
28 Apr 2014

",. Three punctuation marks that pretty much sum up everything in life. First, it begins. It goes on. Then it all ends. But for this shit of Möbius strip, there is no period at the end. I'm getting fed up of feeling fed up (insert tear-your-hair GIF). I threw the *Montblanc* pen on a row of spidery 'h'. *Why am I doing this shit?* There is a time for everything. So get on your way. *Please. Just … don't.* But do what I want, this shitty-as-hell life seems to go on and on.

But there is hope yet.

Good times happen over coffee. And they say time flies when you're having a good time. Maybe I could drink more coffee in the name of fun.

For now, the shit must go on. Life sucks. But so do you. Suck it up!

***

"How do you feel?"

Feel.

I want to feel again. I honestly don't know what I feel now. Many times, before I clamber out of a car, I let the seat belt snap back, my thumb still on the release catch. The buckle hit my heart implant, reminding me hard that nothing feels the same anymore.

Not ever.

Conversations with others often end with over-egging. Cue a forced fist-pumping. Feels fake but okay. What do you expect others to say?

"Good."

#SoDone

Next > **Smile is a good cry in the shower.**

Smile is a good cry in the shower.
09 Jun 2014

Fun fact: Six out of ten people sing in the shower because they know that no one can hear them.

Not me. I cry. One night as my hair trickled to a tip, I held my breath. Then it struck.

The fact that I'm still breathing means I matter to my creator. God still has a purpose for me. I'm not useless after all. I cupped water to my lips, swishing it around. I slathered over puce marks chafed by the crutches. Then I cringed as pain flared and the lather stung. Stubbed my finger up my nose again. The loss of dexterity is crippling. Banal tasks like brushing teeth became agonizing. I began crying.

Crying is no laughing matter. Once a while, me-time is needed to hush all my hurts. Crying is bloodless bleeding. You bleed feelings. Feelings that harden wounds when exposed to time. No Johnny Depp cry on demand though. The heart needs to cry badly but the mind often pushes the tears right back up. Too sad to cry. When tears don't fall, wounds can't heal. I wonder how Sonia cries. God only knows how suffocating that tiny apartment must be.

I had never cried in front of my family. What happens in my mind, stays out of other minds. I have also never cried myself to sleep. Sleep is my only escape.

I sucked in a shaky rush.

#LikeNothingEverHappened

Next > **Life is hard, I shit you not.**

13

Life is hard, I shit you not.
28 Jun 2014

I blew out sharply, sour-breathed.

Uselessness flapped like a bat out of hell as Brother retched. He had gastric flu. And I couldn't do anything for him. Now I know how he felt in the glassed-in intensive care unit. Soon, it's my turn though. One night my eyes tore in bone-chilling horror, utterly petrified. The last time I felt this way is when I nearly missed my flight to Tokyo.

I nuked in my pants.

Scared shitless (or shitful), I yelled for Brother. I limped, painfully slow, with the walker to wash up while he lay a plastic under-sheet. *The stench must have jolted you awake,* Sonia had laughed it off.

Crushed. Absolutely. Crushed by this Bowel Malfunction. Instead of falling asleep, I began falling apart.

***

If a world falls at night and no one is around to hear it, does it make a sound?

On a balmy night after another toilet run, I couldn't go back to sleep. I tossed and mulled over a life teeming with dreariness. Everyone else, it seemed, has a purpose. *What is mine?* I had become a nobody. *What is my reason for existence? Why did God create me?* I lay awake, pelted by whorls of fret as I thought of why my world is what it is. Forced to home in on a new purpose, I struggled to impose a hold on imagination. *What if I can't walk again? What if Sonia leaves me? What if—?* Thinking exposes a moment when you are at your most vulnerable. It is crucial for charting out your next step. Trouble is, you can't unthink and stop from dithering wild.

I turned from the nightlight Mom had plugged in. Then turned again. The jousting match between birds rattled me. As do buses rumbling to life. I listened to the white noise of the neighborhood chugging away. And felt the world of somebodies living without me. As it was, the fear of being alone kept me up into the dawn.

Or was it the fear of being?

#LostToBeFound

Next > **I have no words for this.**

14

I have no words for this.
7 Jul 2014

I don't want to talk about this.

I want to scream.

#HowTheHellDoIKeepCalmAndCarryOn

Next > Just three words.

15

Just three words.
26 Jul 3014

"I only know—", I dabbed my eyes, "—I love you."

I love you.

Three words that riddled like a stubborn earworm. Three words I wanted to tell Sonia and my family. I always believe life is a 'Show N Tell'. You don't just say "I love you". You show it too. Before the stroke, I would make gifts for Sonia. I no longer do that. It's not that I no longer cared. It's just …

… just three words. I can't anymore.

#ActionsLessThanWords

Next > **Crash Test Dummies.**

Crash Test Dummies.
04 Aug 2014

Make it or break it, I shoved my knuckles through the crutches. But sometimes you make it by breaking. Like a crash test dummy. I need to end it with Sonia. She's drifting away. When holding on is the only thing holding back, it's time to let go. Letting go is never easy. It takes two. But I can't force it on her. This is her life and I have no right over it. She has a choice too. After all, we are in this together.

Like two crash test dummies.

#CrashAndBurn

Next > **Blessed are those who don't remember.**

Blessed are those who don't remember.
24 Aug 2014

Three out of four people who experienced a terrifying
event have trouble forgetting. I remember nothing.
Unbelievable how nothing changes everything.

Remembering can be painful. Especially remembering
what you don't *remember* remembering. A friend told
me she was given morphine to help her sleep after her
accident. Doctors are right—morphine numbs all pains.

Even the pain of remembering.

I am spared the memory of a harrowing collapse. I
don't remember the day everything turned to nothing.
My ex-boss, Chew arranged a meet-up with Singapore
Civil Defence Force. The off-duty fireman. The paramedic
biker. The EMT. The chain of survival is perfect. I learned
how the off-duty fireman applied CPR. I learned how the
paramedic biker gave me—in the most literal sense of the
word—the shock of my life. I also learned something else.

A memory never remembered can be painful too.

#RememberingWhatYouShouldForget

Next > **Normal just ain't normal anymore.**

16

Normal just ain't normal anymore.
04 Sep 2014

It is too painful.

No grab bars for me. I just want a normal life. Well, as normal as possible anyway. I peered into the mirror as I edged the bathing stool. Fogged. I palmed a tile and wiped in clunky swipes. I crunched my nose to arch up the glasses. It's hard to do it with numb fingers. You always end up smudging the lense. You can fry an egg, once I had said to Sonia, with the gunk on my face. I came face to face with myself. Gone is the sunshiny swag.

Those eyes.

The pallor of a man who had started to stop existing. Hitching along the living room, I squinted hard into the glistening stipples.

Awkward slouch. Wobbly lumber. An uncanny resemblance.

The Walking Dead was on.

***

I lobbed a T-shirt onto the bed. A crummy army shirt. I had bumped into a neighbor when I was wearing it. "I can't recognize you," he had said. He wasn't the only one. I couldn't recognize myself, even.

I sat on the end of the bed and leaned back with a thud. One handgrip of the elbow crutch prodded my temple like the muzzle of a *Smith & Wesson*. I turned and glared. The elbow crutch is irksome. It's a love-hate relationship. I came across, on *YouTube*, a clip of Cristiano Ronaldo using one. It's funny to see a FIFA World Player pucker into an *ooh* at the sight of a tiny curb. The therapist had advised me to use a motorized wheelchair. Utterly pulverized by the thought of being confined to a wheelchair. I rather brandish two cumbersome crutches. Not snubbing the wheelchair. I only want to be who I was again.

Why do I have to hanker so hard? It can't be that hard, right?

Right?

#MeBeingMe

Next > **Anything but the only thing.**

Anything but the only thing.
16 Sep 2014

Sonia has unfriended me on Facebook. An ache pinched as I thought of her tapping the *Delete* button under our photos. I didn't dare bring this up. She's already having a tough time.

Maybe she wants to break up softly. Or if not, she might have hit *Unfriend* by accident. Or … or maybe it's all the above. Maybe. I shudder to think of breaking up with Sonia. But I thought anyway. I batted around the imaginings and re-imaginings. All of the malevolent ilk. Even so, I can't blame her. We might well be, let's face it, in or near the end of a beautiful coupledom. A last-ditch grasp at a buckling relationship wouldn't do anyone any good. Eventually, someone has to pull the trigger. I'm grateful to Sonia, though. For all the love. And time. She had given me so much time. I could not ask for more. It is useless hoarding memories anyway. A pain-laden reality is enough. If only adversity would cut me some slack. For once. Just this once. A breakup now—heaven forbid— would crumble the very vestige of sanity.

That night, the fluorescent tube in my room died and I sat in the dark. Surrendering to thoughts that sidled for a violent hurtle with whatever else.
Like the flickering light, this could be a whistle blow for things to come.

***

It turned out she unfriended for a good reason. Our photos in Facebook albums are chock-full of happier times. A time when, unbeknown to me, life had been stropping memories to a glint. Bearing the patina of time, these albums had become litanies of sorrow. A pang jagged with a niggling cadence as I clicked on the photo albums. A bevy of swans reminded me of how I kept bashing into a low-hanging door jamb at the Hakone inn. Back when I could still walk. It takes—I now know— indomitable fortitude to pull through this emotional plunder. Sonia and I agreed to work hard, mustering all the strength we need. Life is full of storms. We can't always bask in sunny-side-up days. I had found a girl who would share one umbrella. I felt, more certain than ever, I had found a keeper. Keeping her by my side is something else altogether.
After all, finders might not be keepers.

***

Sonia is not the only girl, I believe, to get an animated emoticon made for her. But it's the best I could do. Staying in love had never been so hard. Way harder than staying alive. There is so much I wanted to do for her. I hung onto every day with the hope that I can make them true one day. My quavering fingers found their way to *Settings*.
And I wonder when would I put my phone to *Airplane mode* again.

#YouCantKeepThoseWhoDontBelongToYou

Next > **This is that.**

This is that.
29 Sep 2014

This. This is that *why*.

Why I don't talk about the days I got shit on my hand as I learned to wipe my ass. Why I don't talk about the nights I peed on myself. Because of this.

Family.

My mind stayed on because of them. Family is a heft from the trauma of life. And you sure can't beat me when it comes to support from the near and dear. Putting food on the table. Bringing in the bathing stool. Everyday struggles are on the verge of tipping my sanity. Tight-knit support talked me off the ledge.

"Wait for me here if you end early," Dad said as he nudged the handbrakes.

***

"Uncle!"

A chunk of flyaways bustled behind the sofa. Sebastian frolicked in a new game that calls for yelling my name and scampering for cover. He comes up with goofball antics every so often.

"You cannot catch me," he said without missing a beat.

I still remember, once, how he yelled, "Uncle!" and scurried to my hospital bed, the moment Brother put him down. And that, I realized then, was also the moment I discovered just how dearly I missed him. And to think I was so close to not hearing him for good. Not everyone deserves to be a second-timer.

Thank God I did.

#OneThingThatWillNeverChange

Next > **Never have I ever.**

17

Never have I ever.
03 Oct 2014

Lost.

One Sunday night, I Skype-d Sonia as usual. And after, alone in the dark, I cried. I hope no one heard my sobs. It pains me to see Sonia so saddled. She deserves better than this bludgeoning. She was always there for me. Which is a remarkable feat for a long-distance relationship. Never in the history of me have I felt this hopeless. Helpless. As never have been. But you can do nothing.

What other choice did I have?

#savage #DownAndMoreDown

Next > **Do you even lift?**

Do you even lift?
05 Oct 2014

Me: Never bow to adversity unless it's to drink coffee.
Also me: Who's cutting onions?

In everyone's life, there's always something said that hurts. For me, it's the unsaid. Some things are better not put in words. One and a half years and counting, I still could not walk. Much to my chagrin, recovery seemed to hit a dead end. The unspeakable crept up. I might never walk again. I seem to be heading nowhere in life but there's nothing I could do.

Or is there?

Scapegoat-christening is a waste of time. I'm a stroke survivor. Not a victim. I refuse to be this tyrant's A-list muse just yet. Forget the letter from *Hogwarts*. There is no magic. I must break free from this chokehold on my own.

The rampage prised an ever widening rift between Sonia and me. The feeling that we are growing apart gnawed away, little by little, from the inside. I kept it from Sonia. But I'm certain that she sensed it too. We are worlds apart now. Not just 3000 miles. The widening gulf badgered me to buck up. Question is, how? There has to be a way. Sonia and I are facing the toughest test. One that battered our lives in one fell swoop. She is leading a normal life. I'm not. That makes me determined to break out of this rotting terrarium. Stuck, day after day, in a limbo of eat, sleep, therapy and repeat. But there must be a way. You can't DNF Life. I had been out of work for two years now. No work and no play makes me a mad boy.

So I approached SPD (formerly Society for Physically Disabled).

#ICantSeeAWay #ButIKnowTheresOne

Next > **Technology is best when you can't do the rest.**

Technology is best when you can't do the rest.
08 Oct 2014

I had been putting this off for the longest of time. A part of me refuse to accept that I am disabled now. From being in love to being in denial. But denial is pointless. The crutches are wearing out. I hovered away to the *Dean & Deluca* website.

The duality of technology is painful. On one hand, technology is nothing short of a godsend for the homebound. Empowering to buy your own things. On the other, the interconnectedness of social media haunts. Sonia and I had already unfriended on Facebook. If only I can meet Sonia for the first time again. But that would also mean we meet our fate all over.

Boo.

Once my iPhone fried after it had a dunk in the toilet bowl. I had just gotten to know Sonia. I couldn't do without my phone. I turned to my only hope. Google. A long-distance relationship has turned me into a hapless digital addict.

No iPhone? How will I live?

I left it in front of the AC overnight. Nothing. The next day—and night for good measure—I stashed it in a bag of rice.

It worked.

All but the Bluetooth and Wi-fi functions came back. No matter. I could fire up *Whatsapp*. That's all I needed to talk to Sonia again.

"You're so lucky," said a buddy.

"Excuse me?"

"There's no shit yet."

He's got a good point. Now I feel how my iPhone must have felt back then.

Only this time, the shit is neck-deep.

***

No copping the drops at ASOS these days but every time the postman rang, I'm more than stoked. It means only one thing. Coffee. Sonia has been sending beans from the finest roasteries like Intelligentsia and Stumptown, getting me all heart-eyed. She also sent a metal disk filter for my AeroPress. It allows more oils to permeate for a full-bodied cup. Perfect for my indulgence.

The only one these days.

#TechnologyCantChangeEverything #LoveCan

Next > **When your dream goes after you.**

18

When your dream goes after you.
11 Oct 2014

Believe in your dreams, no matter how impossible they seem,
said Walt Disney. Thing is, I don't have any now. The
stroke crushed them. Many moons ago, in my half-sleep,
I became a vampire. I sank my incisors, sucking the red
ooze slowly. With every throb, I felt the last smidge of
affliction drain away. I could finally go Tokyo to see
Sonia. I had pursed my lips and ran my tongue over
to smooth the stickiness. Bizarre. Though it was just a
dream, it showed one thing.

I am dead-set to be with Sonia.

#LivingNightmare

Next > **Back to Ground Zero.**

Back to Ground Zero.
05 Nov 2014

Mom handed over an envelope. Now that my eyes have
gotten better, I could read my own letters. The envelope
juddered in my hand as I ripped. It's a means test for state
welfare. I got to declare my income. Easy to fill. A big,
fat zero. I heard my nephew gibbering to the Minions on
YouTube. Only me and Sebastian are jobless in a family of
soon-to-be-seven.

I snorted.

#BeginningAfterTheEnd

Next > **Nerd VS Meathead.**

Nerd VS Meathead.
16 Nov 2014

My physical abilities are now severely limited. But the possibilities of my brain are endless. The brainstem controls critical functions like heartbeat, breathing and swallowing. Brainstem stroke survivors usually have intact cognitive functions. I keep my thinking ability fully. My brain works the way it always has. During rehabilitation, there's a flurry of physical tasks to be relearned. Writing ABCs. Eating with chopsticks. Buttoning a shirt. They piss the hell out of me. Now that my body's broken, shouldn't I use my brain to think more? Why am I not seen to have one? Am I a good-for-nothing just because I had a stroke? How do I turn my crisis into an opportunity? Whatever it is, one thing's for sure.

It's brain over brawn. Mind over matter. Simple, but not easy.

#SmarterNotHarder

Next > Bros before woes.

19

Bros before woes.
20 Nov 2014

I bathed early. Didn't want to hog the bathroom while Brother gets ready for work. Rucking up the sock, I tried to shove my foot in. It skewed and I tugged again. This is the first time I'm meeting the lads outside after the stroke. After the stroke, my social life took a backseat. More like it's all trussed up in the boot.

It is our annual In-Camp Training. Our yearly mandatory call-up like the army. Raucous ribbing welcomed me. The poke-in-the-rib barrage is all too familiar. It seemed as if nothing has changed even though everything did. I clambered sidelong into the passenger seat, narrowly missing my head. "I'll take care of myself," I nodded, secretly wondering how I could do so. But boy oh boy, being alive sure feels good. The lads may be rowdy but their message is clear.

Leave no man behind.

#SquadGoals

Next > **Men of steal.**

Men of steal.
23 Nov 2014

Freedom.

You never know its price until you lose it. Once it's lost, you can never get it back. Even if you sell a kidney. One afternoon an orderly had parked me in front of the TV and left. I whimpered as the tittering motion graphic shredded. Then the Pterodactyl-screaming news ticker drove a stake through. I closed my eyes. At that very moment, a clang pierced. It grew into a rattling. As the rattling got louder, weak shuffles echoed heavy thuds. I need not open my eyes to know that an inmate in a purple jumpsuit had walked by, escorted by two policemen. The hospital is near a prison. Which is worse? Having freedom taken from you or being taken away from freedom?

But I can't stew in bereavement. I refuse to be sniveling in victimhood. Now I can't do simple things—perhaps ever—anymore.

But eh.

Adversity and its exhaustions be damned. Everything seem to have screwed up according to plan. A cruel diversionary ploy. It stopped me dead (half-dead more like it) in my tracks. Why, I was about to gun all cylinders.

During our Tokyo Coffee Trail, we headed to *Bear Pond Espresso*, helmed by the titular Katsuyuki Tanaka. His insouciant—you might even say cavalier—demeanor made it a must-stop. We bought a copy of his book *Bear Pond Espresso*. Tanaka signed off with the message: *Break away from conventional thinking*. It turns out to be so fitting now. For the stroke shunted me in this grueling Cold War.

Disable is not a dirty word. I want to be the *able* in *disable* and turn from a Person with Disability (PWD) to a Person with Determination. Not all PWDs are born. Some are made. For me, it all happened bang overnight. To move forward and onward, I have to look well beyond what I once had and who I once was.

Life is at stake, risk at your own risk.

#swerve #ClapBack

Next > **Heavy mettle.**

Heavy mettle.
25 Nov 2014

On the way to a therapy session, a happy-poppy song
from my fave K-drama played. Raindrops chased down
the misted-up window. A drop streaked and met another.
They sank and perished at the bottom as if all had been
too much to bear. I loved watching raindrops on the
bus window with pitter-patter on the other side. I hadn't
ridden a bus since forever. And how I missed it. A twinge
pricked under my skin. I recognized it as grief only when
it began hurting.

The song that played during the meet-her-folks dinner.

I listened to the blithe banter during my community
walks. Bright tinks from cups and saucers cut the chatter.
Whirs of the coffee grinder. A chime jingled overhead as a
couple stepped out of a shop. The girl looped onto the lad
as they looked down the alley. Just like Sonia and me. I
had brought her to the same shop.

"Look!" She had pointed excitedly.

I craned to see what she was looking at. A coffee pot
molded into a monkey.

"Let's see if there's Doggy too. One for you, one for me."
Doggy wasn't around. Poor Monkey.

Sonia.

What is she doing now? The hustle fell in long
shadows from the other side. The girl smiled. He laughed
back. And they walked across the road. Jealous. I had
long, long forgotten this. As I braced for the lumber back,
suddenly I realize why the chicken crossed the road.

Simply because it can.

#draking #YoungEnoughNotToCare
#DisabledEnoughToKnowBetter

Next > **All the feels ever.**

All the feels ever.
27 Nov 2014

You can too. Feel the smell.

One morning, rubbing with the heels of my hands, I smelled Tokyo. Sonia's home. Lavender. Smells link our feelings to memories. Heaps of memories. Everything we do has got a smell. That's why Sonia let me smell coffee beans when I was in the coma. Smell is a big part of coffee's taste. External smell is when you inhale from the cup. Swallowing sends a burst of aroma up the back of the mouth. That's why a fresh brew smells like heaven.

Keep the coffee game strong. Believe me, you won't regret it.

#TheSmellOfAMemory

Next > **Silence doesn't fall.**

Silence doesn't fall.
02 Dec 2014

It rises.

Faintly at first, then a violent everything at once, until loneliness reeks. Swollen and clammy. On a windless afternoon, Sonia stopped replying to my messages. That night, I lay in the heavy air, listening to the thudding of my heart.

Could it be—

Sonia is just as helpless. If not more so. There's only so much shit she can take. I rolled over and lost my mind trying to find hers. The wrongness … utterly repulsed by this savagery. For something we cannot take rap. But what else can we do? Your life is a work of fate. Any agony to you, living or dead or, worse yet, half-dead, is entirely intentional. That night I didn't ask her why. She knows why. I know why.

We just don't know when.

#WhenLovelessnessTurnsIntoHopelesssness

Next > **All I want for Christmas is us.**

21

All I want for Christmas is us.

13 Dec 2014

1. Super-breathable baseball cap
2. Short sleeve jersey of ultra-breathable mesh
3. Sneakers with highly breathable uppers

#DearSanta

Next > **The year of end.**

22

The year of end.
24 Dec 2014

The party-hearty season rolled around. It's the time of the year I remember how the grinchest Grinch stole my freedom. I laughed at the ruckus as my nephews exchanged gifts with their cousins. Nothing is as contagious as kids' laughter. Or so I thought. One afternoon, Sebastian scrambled after Mom to fix his broken truck. "Very please!" Seeing him all crinkled and sniffling and heaving, my nose puckered and I felt like crying too. So there is something as contagious as kids' laughter after all.

After the stroke, I could no longer usher in the new year at parties. This is the second new year eve I could not count down. Just three years ago, I had counted down with Sonia in a shower of fireworks. The clinks of champagne glasses to ring in the new year. Little did we knew, it would also ring the death knell for my freedom.

The exuberance of parties is a sharp contrast to my despair. SPD organized a party for us. It meant a lot to me as it was my first X'mas celebration after the stroke. An awful lot. It was a simple gathering but even so. When you have nothing, something means everything in the world.

Everything.

***

Auld Lang Syne gets everyone in a pensive mood. I might have turned into the biggest turkey in life but it's okay. After all, tis' the season of (for)giving. As the year shrank in the rear-view mirror, year in review lists abound. Rounding up the highs and lows. World Cup. Ice bucket challenge. Apple Watch. Mine was simple.

Stroke.

#FestiveJeer #DecWrapUp #2014BestPine

Next > Hello, Sylvester.

Hello, Sylvester.
31 Dec 2014

Sylvester Tan
Dec 31st, 2014
10:45 AM
5.3 LBS
15 INCHES
With love, the Tan Family

#PrisonBreak

Next > **Things happen for a reason: me.**

24

Things happen for a reason: me.
03 Jan 2015

While my friends are getting down and dirty, I'm just getting dirty with this shit. Like a destitute dumped by life. Helpless. Shackled to my disabilities, I sought a respite by writing my blog. Writing is a good coping mechanism. Expressing my thoughts is a powerful catharsis.

I couldn't type so iPhone saves the day. Writing on it is a fumble but here's a neat hack. When you've had enough, give up giving up. That way, you can keep on keeping on. God has given me the gift of writing. I'm sure He enjoys watching me use it. It's not underneath the Christmas tree, though. I had to get lost to find it. I never had the desire to write until now. Everything happens for a reason, people say. I don't think so. Things don't always happen for a reason. You have to give it one.

If you can't find any, be one.

#fomo #ItWillAllMakeSense

Next > **The want I never knew I needed.**

The want I never knew I needed.
06 Jan 2015

I went for a walk, one cloudless morning, 650 days after the stroke. The sun beat on the bare path of my old running route. Now here I am, learning how to walk. I still couldn't cross the road in time. I am now NSFW. Not shirking the return to work. I wanted, more than anything, to get back to work. SPD had no luck hunting for home-based employment. I should ask Chew for help. When I was still in coma, he had told Sonia I could work in the agency again. But—

—Bowel Malfunction.

Damn.

I chatted with the social worker. I should feel better.

But I didn't. At all.

#thirsty

Next > **Better things are coming—I hope.**

Better things are coming—I hope.
09 Jan 2015

When in doubt, always choose hope. The afternoon was warm. She was the boss of a social enterprise and we met up at the SPD canteen. I had applied for the position of a home-based graphic designer. She told us about overseeing operations between Cambodia and Singapore.

And what a difference.

She once gave a talk in a building with no lift in Cambodia. A wheelchair-bound girl had to get down and haul herself up the stairs, step by step, to attend. Must have been a crushing sight. Ever since the stroke, I receive everything with gratitude. Ramp. Lift. I can't imagine living without them. Life, as it is, is hard enough.

"My heart—" the lady boss said. "—went out to her."

She knew. For the first time in a long time, I felt understood. God, I don't know what freaking plans you have for me. But I trust you. I trust you.

Let this be good.

#belief

Next > **Kids do the darndest things.**

25

Kids do the darndest things.
08 Feb 2015

A good life makes you laugh a lot.

I discovered the 10th planet. Or at least its inhabitants. One afternoon Sylvester was in the middle of a fashion show with yet another romper change. I caught Sebastian flapping his arms wildly while marching to the shiny fridge, holding two books. "I want to fly," he huffed and puffed. Sebastian turned and flapped even harder. I laughed. They are happiness that smile back, kids. Perhaps someday I'll have my own. Someday. Some other day.

Just not today.

#TheyWillChangeTheWorld

Next > **A little now and then.**

A little now and then.
23 Apr 2015

All is fair in love and war. But life?

Life is not fair. It is great—when you least expect. As my thumb ran across the Angry Bird keychain on Sebastian's school bag, I looked at his toys strewn. A few days ago, his tooth fell off in school. He waggled the wad, eager to share his excitement, and declared that it would be his Mother's Day gift. Moments like this makes life that little bit better. They remind me to keep living a life worth living.

And living is what life is all about.

I chuckled as he monkeyed on the couch, snuggling a pillow. A nape wiggled like a kitty's scruff. He is so happy it makes me happy. He had a big head and no neck as a toddler. I would ask him to clasp his hands overhead and laugh at his futile attempts. The moment is over too soon but, hey. With kids, there's always another. I totally need this in my life right now. I had been indifferent towards kids but the little tykes have changed me. Changed the way I look at things. Sebastian once knelt on a chair, perched his cup on the table. He flounced off, hop-skippity, wheedling for ice-cream. Moments like this do wonders to the deadness of my struggles. Sometimes, I even enjoyed myself. Few things in life are more fun and funny than kids. They never fail to cheer me up in this plunder.

One night, Dad was preparing for a fishing trip when Sebastian scurried up with toy scissors and an offer to help. I smiled as Brother walked past and chided him for interrupting. Life gave me much to be thankful for.

What a time to be alive!

#TeachThemAllAboutLife #LearnAllLifeIsAbout

Next > **Tender is my might.**

Tender is my might.
02 May 2015

My stroke is two-sided indeed. The tenderest brutality of vagary. A joy rose as Mom dandled Sylvester in a peek-a-boo. Sylvester looks like my sister-in-law turned into a Minion. I always greet him with "Hello, hello." Cherish your hello because you might never get a chance for goodbye. I feel so grateful every time the cinnamon roll cries. My favorite little sunshine. The babbling violent objections. The older munchkin squealed over the ping and buzz of *Nickelodeon*. And right then, with freakish suddenness, I did what I did.

I cried.

#MicDrop

Next > **When love falls, pain calls.**

26

When love falls, pain calls.
10 May 2015

Love conquers all.

All but a stroke.

Two years after the stroke, Sonia and I broke up. For all her patience, I knew this day would come. Her patience—much like everything else—runs out after a while. No force on earth can salvage love after it's gone. There's no need to hack *Ashley Madison* to know Love has cheated on us. There is no point pulling together our wilting relationship, even trying. Love just isn't there anymore. Unloveness bled us dry as we drew on. My disabilities meant the end of little zingers that keep a long distance relationship alive. The snap of our skies every day. The little gifts. The reasons to stay.

We put up a valiant fight. But in the end, the only things that broke are our hearts. And I only know one way to nurse a heartache. Coffee. More coffee. Only coffee. As I sipped the beans from Sonia, I remembered her words and felt hurt for feeling relieved. A strange benumbing. An agonizing relief, somehow freed.

If you look at Maslow's hierarchy of needs, I had fallen from the rungs of happiness. I have to start with basic physiological ones, putting settling down on the back burner till God only knows when. She is, more ready than ever, about to move into the fourth level—esteem needs of love and belonging. I'm not saying Sonia would not have a future with me, but as it is now, I would take years to get to anywhere near where she is. If I do at all. There is simply too much between Sonia and I. It scares me to lose Sonia. But if I can't have her, I need to let go and free her. When Life breaks you, only one thing is left to hold on. Your own breath. The one God gave you.

If I am not the half who could make her whole, I can't
stop her search for happiness. It's been two years and I
seemed to have dead-ended. I still cannot cross the road.
I still can't blow my nose without getting snot all over like
nattō strings. Our lifestyles drove a ever-growing wedge
between us. We are worlds apart now. Not just continents.
In all probability—one chance in a billion—there is
no other long distance relationship quite like ours. Our
crash-and-burn coupledom is as romantic as they come.
Made all the more unforgettable by the fact that it all
began on *Instagram*. Unforgettable in so many ways.
The fluttering on *Instagram*. The cavorting in cafe crawls.
The stuff of dreams. But nothing lasts forever and all
good things must come to an end.

I would never have imagined ending with a "it's not
you, it's me." Not by a long, long stretch. Then again, I
would never imagine our forever to be four years and six
months. But that's just the way life is. I had a happy time.
A once-in-a-lifetime kind of happy. I hoped she was happy
too. With this, I bagged bragging rights to surviving
a holocaust of love. One I could regale endlessly at
an old-age home.

I have nothing but thanks for Sonia. She has given her
all. Not only did she wait for me, but Sonia had done so
much—too much, I think sometimes—for me. The coffee
beans. The little knick-knacks and suchlike. It would be
ungrateful to ask for anything more. She gave us everything
she could. Nothing's left. Not anything more, really. And
Sonia didn't leave me suddenly, unexpectedly. The stars
didn't align—one true pairing turns out to be untrue—so
we shear off in separate ways. Anyway, this is the end of a
relationship. Not my life. As for how life could go on without
Sonia, I have no idea, God bless me. I just know it has to.

And it will.

#PromisesCanBeBroken #NotHearts

Next > **Close encounters of the kind.**

Close encounters of the kind.
03 Jun 2015

I tugged the zip. My favorite windbreaker. I had bought it
in Ginza. The elevator doors began to shut and I prodded
them with my crutches. *I'm getting good at this.* I hitched
around to thumb the buttons. When the door opened
again later, he is right there. The driver from SPD. He was
waiting for me at the lobby. It had been raining and he
arranged a different pickup point. He shielded me with
an umbrella and lent his arm for support. I smiled and
nodded my thank-you.

But not all are that understanding. I don't lock toilet
doors anymore for fear of a collapse again. After an
outpatient therapy session, I went to the toilet. As usual,
I didn't lock. Not knowing it was occupied, a woman
barged in. I heard her lashing out as I was peeing. I
then limped out, smirking at how pissed (see what I did
there) she was. Sorry not sorry. But most are forgiving.
These days, I'm grateful—even touched by kindness,
however random. Once, I was walking along the lobby
when a group of young people came to sing carols. One
of them left the group to sit on a bench near me. He sat,
leaning forward with hands clasped in front of his knees.
Sometimes he leaned back and watched. After a while, he
came up to me.

"May I pray for you?" As he laid his hand on my
shoulder, I thank God. Before we come from our mothers'
tummies, we come from His heart.

A little kindness goes a long way. Long enough, I
hope, to get me through this misery.

#YouDontNeedAReasonToHelpOthers

Next > If it were us.

If it were us.
5 Jun 2015

I miss walking. I miss working. And I miss Sonia so much.
    I struggled to sop the gunk off my chambray shirt. The groom and bride began long-distance dating just as Sonia and I did. I remember how we exchanged tips for long-distance dating. How we talked about plans for the future. Before this shit stuck a needle in my balloon. The banter with so many former colleagues reminded me of good old times. When it ended, one of them offered a ride back. Suddenly I wish it's Marty McFly's wheeled time machine. "What would you have done differently if you can turn back the clock?" Chew had always asked me. Nothing. Wouldn't change a thing. If I knew then what I know now, would I know better?
    Usually I would gussy up for a wedding. The stroke had forced me to shed *Hypebeast* trappings. And it shows. Unkempt hair. It's hard to get to the hairdresser's. Or anywhere, for the matter. And the last time I checked, they do not have any plans of getting a helipad. My crowning glory is, indeed, glorious. To make my haircut last, I keep the tuft on top and asked for sides and back to be shaven. A coiff Dear Leader would have approved.
    After the dinner, I asked for coffee—hoping it might be easier to forgive life.

#ratchet

Next > **The most impossible of possibilities.**

27

The most impossible of possibilities.
6 Jun 2015

Forgive and forget.

One does not simply forgive and forget. You need a reason to forgive. But sometimes to forgive *is* the reason. And this reason can't exist in a monstrous plume of *hows*.

How can you forgive when no one is in the wrong? How can you forget when someone is in your heart?

PS. I had kept empty coffee bean packages from Sonia. Wanted to put together a 'thank-you' photo-collage. A month after we broke up, I got Mom to throw everything.

The futility of it all painfully realized.

***

Some days are kinder. It might seem like a fruitless dalliance in the end but it's sweet that we tried. It had been a good run. Just not a home run. Painful as it might be, I never wish to hit *Backspace*. Once Sebastian stubbornly refused a giveaway balloon. He didn't want to be sad when it goes all limp. I would take it even if I know Life is going to prick it one day. I have no regrets, knowing it had made me happy once.

Forever is the perfect happiness because it doesn't exist.

I mulled over this collateral damage. One that left nothing but nameless memories. Memories that we remember in all their Technicolor delight. Now, try and try as I might, I can't throw them out. The unforgettable is unforgiving. It is cruel how the memories that we feel about most care least. Memories sidled to taunt me every night with a brutal playlist. The worst is no proton pack can exorcise them. I felt a burgeoning breathlessness creeping up. The second time in as many days. I limped to my room to read an eBook. As I picked up the iPad, I wonder what goes through Sonia's mind as she throws away our sepia-toned tenderness. There are two sides to the same story. How are things on her side?

I began reading about high school sweethearts as the galaxy went on bursting with emptiness.

#FirstToForgive #LastToForget

Next > **Be alive. Or die trying.**

Be alive. Or die trying.
08 Jun 2015

We would love to work with you again.
No. Not again.
Another slim chance had just become fat hope. And no news from the lady boss. And no news from other employers. And *hurt*. Hurt is expecting a rejection but not getting a reply at all. What hurting. Hurting this much hurts. I came back for Life and this is what I get? My heart crumpled and I hunkered down for a barrage. Shallowness racked. I ran out of breath while breathing. Like my veins suddenly hardened into scars under my skin. Coldness bristled down my neck as a flush sloshed up my throat. Like my first night in Tokyo. Only this time, it hurts. The outbreak throbbed through my bones. All 206 of them.

I miss the daily grind. Ah yes, the grind. How I miss being under the sheets. Spreadsheets, I mean. #ManCrushMonday. #TransformationTuesday. #WomanCrushWednesday. #ThrowbackThursday. #FlashBackFriday. This all means little to nothing for me. I lost my reason for living. I love drawing. But I can no longer hold a pencil. I love design. But I can no longer use the mouse. I love swimming. But I can no longer walk.

Look at me. I can't tell which is more hopeless. Losing everything you have. Or losing everything you know. Or … losing everything you never knew you had. But I still believe in God's plan. If you don't know where you are, follow GPS. God's Positioning System. Your situation is not your destination. I told Sonia that the job trial didn't work out. She didn't ask why. She just said we were not fated to be together. A sinking feeling rose. Could this be a subtle hint? Maybe it's just me getting touchy.

Or not.

#TheStrawThatBrokeMe

Next > **What might have been …**

What might have been …
17 Jun 2015

We. Might. Have.

Three words that festered in a breathlessness so deep, lungfuls of air can't fill. It feels like trying to breathe through Cling Wrap. Choked up with every drag. To stop the thin film from smothering, all you can do is keep breathing out and breathing out.

And breathing out still.

Memory is the heaven for love. But when love dies, it's hell for you. *Why don't I run out of memory now?* I squeezed my eyes tight as a rush flared. And my, this feeling can be triggered and re-triggered by every little thing. There was this one time I was flipping the papers when I came across a movie review on an upcoming Steve Jobs biopic. The first time I went to Tokyo. I was with Sonia when news of his death broke. I remember how I felt indebted to him as I would never have met Sonia without *Apple* (*Instagram* was still an iPhone-only app). God only knows what might happen if I didn't get a stroke.

We might have.

Of course we would have. But I would never know. And I would always wonder in this lifetime of ever. I did not cry when we broke up. I found it strangely numbing. All too numbing, even calming. As if pain itself is a narcotic. I couldn't even feel. Let alone think and cry. In fact many times, I tried to bawl my eyes out, hoping to cry until I unexist. But no tears.

Only fears.

#WhatMightBe

Next > **The saddest things in life aren't things.**

28

The saddest things in life aren't things.
19 Jun 2015

A picture paints a thousand words. And only one story.

The story of what will never be.

I blew on a dust-choked strip of photos. I remember the togetherness as Sonia and I huddled close, oblivious to the world. Oblivious to how falling from heaven would hurt like hell. Once upon a life I had fallen madly in love.

Had.

Now I'm only mad. So think twice before falling madly in love. Love comes and goes. But you will be mad forever. A *Dean & Deluca* fridge magnet. A *Uniqlo* T-shirt. A *Lonely Planet* Pocket Tokyo travel guide. What makes a breakup painful is not absence but presence. These keepsakes marked the passing of happiness. Putrefying grave markers in an abandoned amusement park. They used to have so much pride of place. I laid the keepsakes in a black box, right by the Monkey coffee pot. I keep them, ready to forget, but it doesn't help, really. The harder I try to forget, the more I would remember.

I picked up the photo frame beside. Wistfulness closed in. In the family portrait taken during Brother's wedding from forever ago, there was a young man who was me. One night Sebastian had scudded into my room, and perched on my bed. His eyes swiveled around the room and landed on that photo. He then demanded to know, arms akimbo, why was he not in it. I laughed as I hemmed and hawed. It was at that moment when I wondered where is the young man now. And I felt sad.

Because he looked so damn good in the gingham shirt.

#MemoriesAreFleeting #PicturesAreWeeping

Next > **When sickness becomes a thing of the young**

When sickness becomes a thing of the young.
23 Jun 2015

Why did I have a stroke?
Oh right, just because.
     Think the so-damning-it-didn't-need-to-be-spelled S-word is an old geezer's affliction? Think again. Take a good look at me. Having a stroke soon after hitting the big three-o smushed the fallacy. Physical exercise is touted as the best way to recover but I disagree. Nothing I do is ever enough. Unsolicited but well-intentioned advice flew from everywhere. I started taking walks around the block if only because I wanted to allay Dad's worries. I feel him.
     But who feels me?

#GOAT

Next > Not all heroes wear capes.

Not all heroes wear capes.
01 Aug 2015

Today is Nurses' Day. As a kid, I grew up with no hero or idolatry. Now, at 35, I have not-so-tender memories of nurses' tender care.
     Memories of how they bathed me. Memories of how they fed me. Memories of how they changed my diapers (thanks for covering my ass). Why is it so hard to forget? Hate this feeling. Anyway, I still have no hero. But I do have many thanks.
     Happy Nurses' Day.

#Thanks #AndEverThanks

Next > Life is a choice. Make it.

Life is a choice. Make it.
11 Sep 2015

Polling Day. Bring out the bubbly. This would be the first time I'm voting as a disabled citizen. Brother fetched me to the polling station. Otherwise I would reach just in time for the next election. This year, the election is greatly divisive. Between hobnobbing in a clubbing VIP queue to voting priority queue for the disabled. Life is a democracy. You don't get to elect the adversity. But how you face it is a choice. Choose wisely.

Don't say I didn't warn you.

#LiveByChoice #NotByChance

Next > **Remedy for a broken heart.**

29

Remedy for a broken heart.
13 Sep 2015

    1. Breathe in
    2. Breathe out
    3. Coffee
    4. Repeat

#FixingABrokenHeart

Next > My heart will go on.

30

My heart will go on.
16 Sep 2015

In the small world that is my life now, I ran into an army mate at the hospital. He took the day off to bring his father for a checkup.

"You're alone?"

"My dad brought me here," I told him with a twinge of guilt. Once, a friend had told me that Life is like a leaf on the tree. It falls off according to seasons. It might also be shed during storms. Some leaves fall when they are still green. Same for Life. Sometimes it ends prematurely because of illnesses and accidents. Nothing can stop it. The analogy made me feel less guilty. But it also made me wonder more.

When will this storm be over?

***

My eyes flickered to life. I squirmed as the icy gel smeared. While my friends are bursting with pride, watching their wives do ultrasound scans, here I am, doing one for my heart. *Plop. Plop. Plop.* I shut my eyes and listened to the *squish* as the lab technician probed like sonar surveillance on the barren sea floor.

As a little boy, I nearly drowned. I had lied to Mom about an excursion to the beach. I rented an Aqua Cycle with cheerful yellow wheels. Parrying the glare, I spotted an overhanging breakwater. Land ahoy! I pedalled furiously, steering towards it. Bumping on the rocks, I leaned over and loped across. The slithery rocks gave way and I fell into the teeming waves.

I couldn't swim. Thrashing wildly, I bobbed for a break, breathing in snatches of burn. I battered, grabbing the dark. All had seemed so sunny a moment ago.

Glimpses of yellow.

This time, my hands found something. I clung on, quaking hard as the lifeguard scooped me. Today I can swim, yet I drown. Water fills the heart. When it breaks, you drown.

Still waters run deep.

#HoldTheTears #DrownTheHeart

Next > **Let it be.**

Let it be.
25 Sep 2015

"Can I have this?" Sebastian held up a twisted loop.
I looked right at it. A wire twirled into Sonia's ring size.
Chucking my luggage, I had placed it against the *Tiffany & Co* Ring Finder app to determine its size.
I remember how I carefully kept it from the nosy boy's reach. I remember racking my brain for ideas to pop the big question. I remember the time we didn't say I do.
Memories. Why didn't I remember to forget?
I said nothing. Sometimes saying nothing at all beats saying something. Because it tells everything I can't say. I looked away and nodded.
A smirk broke as Sebastian unwound it before scurrying away.

#HappyProposeDay

Next > **Love and be loved.**

Love and be loved.
27 Sep 2015

My speech is slurred. Not shaken. Nothing debonair
about it but not all are bothered. Ever so frisky, that
Sebastian, he hardly stop his chittering with me. My
gravelly rasps didn't faze him. One evening, he jiggered,
twinkly-eyed, a *Pocky* stick and last crumbs on his lips
and a new head bump. *Have one,* his smirk beamed, *it's
yummy.* Only then did I see it.

The curly lashes.

I watched him watch SpongeBob SquarePants goggle-
eyed. SpongeBob and Patrick heard a bright chirping. It
was a baby scallop. They adopted him with SpongeBob as
Mom and Patrick as Dad.

Where did the baby that was Sebastian go?

He was growing so fast. Like, he couldn't wait. Often,
you're busy with life and didn't realize that the kids had
stopped being kids. These days, I rarely watch drama.
Who needs *Netflix* with all this action in real life? I
low-key love watching cartoons. It's my way of spending
time with Sebastian. The upside after having a stroke is
that you learn to truly appreciate who you have. Cherish
them today.

What if *you* are gone tomorrow?

#ItTakesSicknessToGrowUp

Next > **The higher you go, the harder you fall and fall.**

31

The higher you go, the harder you fall and fall.
30 Sep 2015

Fallible.

When infallible isn't. Where Sonia and I shouldn't. Why love can't. When l(ove) falls from your world, all that will be left is a word. And the word, for me, is *why*. I would always remember the night we called it a day. Nothing in the world hurts deeper than breaking up over the phone. Because there is no truth to be grasped. As if nothing is real.

As if.

"I need to tell you something." At last. I let up a shuddery squirm. It's happening. Being right never felt so wrong.

"I'm sorry." I kept quiet. You can hear the world on my shoulder fall. My legs swung over. "I'm sorry. We can't go on like this."

I kept quiet still.

"Sorry for being so selfish."

"Don't say—"

What else do you want her to say? "I'm the selfish one." Words spilled out before the corkscrew wrenched my heart along.

"Sorry—sorry … please take care. Get well soon, okay?"

"Thanks … for everything," I said, mostly to myself. *Gotta keep this from Mom. At least for today. It's Mother's Day after all.*

Surprisingly it did not crumble my sanity all at once. It eroded slowly, surely, tearing me to shreds over the days to come. For nights on end, sleep eluded with stubbornness. Memories taunted with searing afterimages. I closed my eyes and stared at them. An unsettledness grew with every toss and turn as I wonder is that all there is.

I deserve the world. Just not this shattered one.

#ShatteredWorldProblem

Next > **The Force didn't awaken.**

The Force didn't awaken.
08 Oct 2015

The old man stopped. He palmed a pillar and heaved, his wife holding on gently. After a while they turned back, presumably heading home to play with their grandkids.

Me? I have nothing.

No money. No honey. Only a shitload baloney. And this sudden urge to shriek.

Exasperated, I hitched around and sat on a park bench. Something was just not right. But on the other hand, nothing was wrong. I looked up at the cottony wisps in deep blues.

Blues that make you happy. Blues that make you happy to be alive.

A fly buzzed around my ear. I tried hard to will it away. It didn't feel it. The fly and I watched a jogger pounding away on the tarmac. I wonder where he's heading, leaning back to rest my head. As I walked back, I caught myself on a window pane. The man in it looked so … different. The wince. The mopey slouch. As if his shoulders are buckling under the misery.

As if feeling how it felt when everything fell apart has changed him forever.

#MayTheForceBeWithMe

Next > The struggle is real.

The struggle is real.
14 Oct 2015

The thing about therapy at SPD—it's heartbreaking. You don't feel sorry for yourself but can't help feeling sorry for others like yourself. Seeing someone as broken as me breaks me. One moment my friends and I are chatting about last night's football match. The next, they struggle to flip the newspaper during therapy.

Jarring. All the hopes undreamed.

But not all is doom and gloom. Banter with therapists offers a much-needed reprieve. Quibbles make therapy sessions less of a dread. These help to brace the—so damn agonizing—uselessness of becoming disabled.

***

On days without therapy, I would head to the stairwell for exercise. Partway up the steps—through the honeycomb grille—I could see a new block of apartment being erected. It grew taller day by day. I wondered when I would finish rebuilding, if ever, a world that toppled like a house of cards. But no one, mind you, no one could answer this question, I thought as my white-knuckled grasp slid down the grimy handrail.

Not myself, even.

***

One afternoon at SPD, I saw a teenager get into a taxi. One of those things I wish I could unsee as I watched. His helper slipped the side panel from his wheelchair and lay it on the road. Her hands slid under the crook of his arms. She then steadied her feet and hauled. When the teenager settled on the seat, he reached for his legs and shoved them across. His helper fixed the panel and wheeled to the boot where the driver was waiting. In the past, I knew nothing about how the others had to deal with everyday struggles. But now, I do. I really do.

I know better.

Something can be learned from everything. There must be a way to parlay my experience and moult into a better being. One who could face the world harder, faster and stronger. I learned the hard way, when adversity hits close to home. A little too close. Hopefully it's just a one-hit wonder.

Only good things come in pairs.

***

I tucked my legs and thrust my clammy fingers and huddled my butt over. I thought of the teenager I saw this afternoon. I feel shitty, sure enough. But when the going gets shitty, the shitty gets going.

I wondered if this is everything to life before darkness subsumed.

#GloUp #woke

Next > **Two words with the most painful possibilities.**

32

Two words with the most painful possibilities.
23 Oct 2015

Sometimes I wonder if Sonia and I would still be together were we not 3000 miles apart. My employment officer goes on wheelchair dates with her able-bodied boyfriend. He would use a wheelchair too to spare her from being talked down to. What if Sonia had been here. The way she looks. The way she laughs. The way she touches.

The way we will never be again.

Sonia has done so much for me. I wonder what she would have done had she been here. But there again … nothing matters anymore.

What if.

#regret

Next > **The mind that wanders off the edge.**

The mind that wanders off the edge.
27 Oct 2015

<u>Word of the Night</u>

Gnaw (v)
The feeling of listening to your circadian rhythm.

Cornered by the scary thought that the future could already be here, I kept thinking of the past. Mom is turning 60 in a couple of months and Dad is already 62. I have never been good with figures (I would love a better grasp of 36-24-36) but I know what this means. Time is ticking away. My head caromed with every wringing *how-now*, each taunting in its own *why*. I kept undeciding what I had decided. Leading me everywhere but mostly nowhere. One stuffy night. I swiped the weather app after

reading old conversations with Sonia. 30 Deg. I wish
Singapore has changing seasons. Crunchy red leaves.
It has always been Fall in love. Never sweet Summer.
I swiped again. Tokyo weather updates. I don't need
it anymore.

As night scumbled into the coming of day, a pall
dappled. Another day, another shit. I better scrounge some
shuteye. This latest bout of insomnia means my standing
balance would be out of whack tomorrow. Lonesome and
tiresome. They simply can't wait to swallow you whole.
Nothing says lonely like listening to squabbling strays at
4:30 a.m, thinking: what good does it do being in love?
Never had I known such loneliness. Where is Morpheus
when you need him?

My friend taught me a relaxation technique. Imagine
water falling, falling, falling between your brows,
spreading out in rings. I turned and one or three drops
streaked down.

Bitter. And something else …

Cry inside and your tears will never dry. Only to be
roiled from the deep each time you remember.

… Sour.

A life gone sour.

#DearSleep #IMissYou

Next > **Play is learning to learn.**

Play is learning to learn.
30 Oct 2015

Some evenings, I would limp to the living room and read
the newspapers again, just so that I could watch Sebastian
eat. Sometimes Mom would be feeding Sylvester too. You
see the slow budding of a 5-month-old to a 5-year-old.
So lucky to live in the same time as the boys are growing
up. You hear the gurgling as baby Sylvester sucked away
and the clanging of spoon as Sebastian ate. I peered like
a fly on the wall, marvelling at how far along the little
tyke has come. All of a sudden, he didn't seem so little
anymore. Kids. So much love fills their hearts, there is no
room for emptiness.
　　No room in theirs. And no room in yours.

#FeelEverything

Next > … of lies and man.

… of lies and man.
31 Oct 2015

"Let me tell you," said Sebastian and his fire truck, all red-eared and crinkled and bubbling snot. "Teacher gave me wafers and I finished them," he continued between sniffles. "Can you go and buy for me now?" he asked, still red-eared and crinkled and bubbling snot.

I looked at his chocolate ringed lips as I muffled.

"Yes," I replied.

Though, I know I can't.

I am no longer a man. Just a grown-up child. A child who doesn't want to tell the truth because it hurts. I *need* to get back to work. Back in the game. A job isn't just a job. It is a reason.

The reason for being.

#WhyExist

Next > **It is what it is. Move on.**

It is what it is. Move on.
01 Nov 2015

Shit. I got that effect on Life.

The good news is, you can grow flowers—or rather, in my case, trees—out of it. I laid my heart out there and life clomped all over. But this time, I must put aside emotions and listen to my head. In the face of this wrecking ball, I have to be proactive, not reactive. No inspire-your-ass-off guru here but I know an opportunity when I see one. To turn the stroke into a wellspring. If I stand a chance—just one last chance—to redeem myself, this would be it. I need to get my shit together and turn the most painful chapter of my life into a watershed period. Being bitter is not going to help. Who says bad things can't happen to good people?

Look at Jesus.

#ThrowingShade #FOH #ShitHappens #DealWithIt

Next > **The not-so-incredible Hulk**

The not-so-incredible Hulk
09 Nov 2015

What would you do when you face a crazy-ass adversary?
    A. Make yourself look bigger
    B. Pretend to drop dead
    C. Run
    My answer: Play dead and sleep my ass off for five days.

But life doesn't always give us a choice. Even if it does, there's a good chance you face the lesser of two evils. I decided to undergo the Radioactive Iodine (RAI) treatment for my hyperthyroid condition. The thyroid gland absorbs all iodine in the body. When radioactive iodine, also known as I-131 (My favorite bus. It trawls the CBD, perfect for ogling office babes) is taken, it concentrates in thyroid cells. The radiation destroys the overactive thyroid gland and you need replacement hormones for life. The treatment might also cause bulging eyes so I could end up looking like Kermit the Frog. If I do, please pass my number to Miss Piggy. I surely stand a decent chance now.

There is no cure for Graves' Disease. Because it doesn't need one. You don't cure sickness to go on living. Sickness is the cure for unlived lives. Today, 09 Nov, is a 911 of sorts. Dad had brought me to the hospital for RAI. The counter chimed. Still a long way to go. My eyes wandered off and saw a woman with perched sunnies. She accompanied her mother. As my sight settled on her Peter Pan collar, her phone rang. She brushed her hair behind the ear and I caught a glimmer. I reached over my ear to feel a prick that was no longer there.

I had a diamond stud too. When they sent me to the ICU, the nurses handed it to Mom and Dad. I dare not ask for it. They were probably too distraught to remember where they kept it anyway. God only knows what they had gone through.

"I'll be back at the office around 2:30 and—", said the woman with the Peter Pan collar. I cursed under my breath for not making out the rest. As if she could hear me, she put the phone away in her beaded clutch and fiddled with her iPad.

It seems so familiar. Not too long ago, I was saying the same thing, along with a perched Aviator.

Now I wonder when I will go back to the office.

The counter chimed again. The woman got up and wheeled her mother to the toilet just as Dad pushed me to the clinical room.

Before I drank, I took one last look at the vial. No gurgling green goo. No technicians in shiny hazmat suits and tongs (I know what you're thinking. Head to Agent Provocateur for those). Imagine such a lifeless fluid can be so ruthless. As I sucked through the straw, I wonder if they got the dosage right. I don't wish to turn into the Hulk. The consequence is unimaginable.

What would happen to my skinny jeans?

#ButWell

Next > **Life is an aftertaste. Not an aftermath.**

34

Life is an aftertaste. Not an aftermath.
14 Nov 2015

Nothing. Everything of nothing ever happens.

Smooth, carefree, lucky—that's how I lived before the stroke. What about life now? Life is an aftertaste. Bittersweet.

Life, now, is busting out chuckles when Sebastian prattles about the mosquito that opened his socks to sting him. Life after a stroke is seeing Sylvester drum with duck lips.

The life I haven't lived.

I am not sure what is worth dying for. But I sure as hell found out what makes life worth living. My life didn't go as planned. But that's okay. I'm sure God's plan is way better. And besides, when times are hard, moments are tender.

Cherish them.

#Life #AcceptIt

Next > **The secret to happiness.**

The secret to happiness.
17 Nov 2015

Reminder to self: Happiness—or at least not being sad—should be the only KPI for life. Life is not a destination. Neither is it about the journey. It's about the person in the driving seat. And how he can be happy.

The secret to being happy is more acceptance, less expectation. Expect less. If this is God's plan for you, so be it. Accept your faith, not your fate. Just take life for what it is, expect zilch in return and you would not be tormented by ought-tos. Even if you can't be happy, it will make you less sad. Hand over all your feelings.

Lord, not load.

#HappinessIsAChoice

Next > **The time is write.**

The time is write.
20 Nov 2015

Que Sera, Sera. Whatever will be, will be.

Writing is speaking with my fingers. Words always sound better coming from my hands. If writing is a gift from God, I'm going to write my ass off. I want to write about a fallen man and his unfallen story. When Life crushes your masterplan, make Plan B. There are 25 more alphabets. And Plan B is a no-brainer.

B for Book.

Writing a book would be impossibly difficult. But impossibly difficult doesn't mean impossible. Anyway, nothing has been easy after I woke. Life can take away my dreams. But never my spirit. I can't walk but nothing can stop me from a leap of faith. God wouldn't bring me this far only to leave me now.

Because whatever will be, will be.

#Difference #AcceptingAndGivingUp

Next > **WANTED: VORACIOUS BIBLIOPHILE**

35

WANTED: VORACIOUS BIBLIOPHILE

30 Nov 2015

SUSPECT INFORMATION
Name: MELVIN TAN
Age: 35 going on 33
Sex: It's been quite a while
Race: CHINESE
Height: 6 FT
Weight: 149 POUNDS
Hair: BLACK
Eyes: TIRED

#WantedDeadOrAlive

Next > **The purpose of work is a work of purpose.**

36

The purpose of work is a work of purpose.
04 Dec 2015

The idea that one needs to be able-bodied to make a living has more holes than Swiss cheese. I'm sure I can eke a living from writing. Chew offered me a copywriting position at the agency. I have been out of work for three years. Busy doing nothing. Going back to the agency is nothing short of a Spice Girls reunion. The comeback of a lifetime.

For someone who only reads coffee bean labels, writing a memoir is a tall order. Luckily Chew pulled together a band of backers. I don't have to tout on Indiegogo to find kickstarters for my life. They would take care of pretty much everything in between while I focus on writing the book. Pursuing a goal requires a reason for being. Breathing new life into my life. Writing a book is just that.

How sad would be 2016 if I'm Unemployee of the Year again.

#StartOver

Next > **When one door closes, another opens.**

When one door closes, another opens.
07 Dec 2015

This is a leap year. I have one extra day to write. I am duty-bound to write a good book. A great one, in fact, to prove my worth. What people have done for, and with me is incredibly inspiring. My family. My friends. My bosses. And I ought to share the experience. A book is a good way to speak out as a second-timer. During a discussion I told Chew I needed more time for the book. Concerned, he asked if I needed a time extension of our back-to-work plan. I wanted to start on the agreed day. I've had enough. This life of same-old-same-old. Okay, he said, without batting an eyelid. Life has driven me up the wall. But he tells me one thing.

His door is always open. Now and always.

#SaveMe

Next > **Learn to live. Live to learn.**

Learn to live. Live to learn.
09 Feb 2016

Is Life done yet?

2016 will be the Year of the Monkey according to the Chinese almanac. Each horoscope cycle comprises 12 animals. Sonia was born in the year of the Dog. I am a Monkey. This will be my third cycle.

Will it ever be my turn, I thought as I stuffed the red packet in my pouch. During Chinese New Year, a red envelope containing money is given by married family and friends for good luck. Family and friends. People who will always be there for you. My favorite people in the world.

With my awful balance, ride-hailing is out. The lads gave me a ride to our Chinese New Year get-together. I watched their part-time hobbits squeal, dodging their Moms around the play tent. One of the girls scuttled behind the canvas when she heard her Mom, holding a candy-colored telephone hostage. Just when her Mom was about to get to her, she scrambled into it. As her Mom knelt by the flap, she scampered out and clambered onto a sofa. From a two-month-old to an eight-year-old, I saw the budding of kids. Remarkable. They will hitso many milestones in life. I thought of Sebastian and Sylvester. I'm so happy to be around to see them grow up, the little rascals. Every day is the childhood they will remember. I wonder if Sebastian will remember how was I like before the stroke.

Will he?

***

"This Wing Chun dealing stance's gonna unleash the Midas touch. Bring it on!"

Blackjack is the game du jour for Chinese New Year. I sat out. I have already lost the biggest gamble of them all—life. Lost in a double-or-nothing wager. But on second thoughts, losing is impossible. You are the only player. When you don't win, you learn. Here's the catch. No learning curve.

Life is the greatest teacher.

#LifeNeverStopsTeaching

Next > Write off the pain.

37

Write off the pain.
17 Feb 2016

Work—we see it as a career or calling. I have found my calling.

Or rather, it has found me. Called to write.

A chance to make up with Life doesn't always come along. Better kiss and tell. Tell the story of a life I almost never lived.

With my speech impairment, writing a book is the only way to tell the story of how Sonia and I were hurled into a world ripped asunder. Life is a torn book, not an open one. Write in the missing chapters. No right or wrong.

Just write.

I never deleted Facebook albums. They are going to come in handy when I write my book. It won't be easy. Last dregs of memories hauled in from my TBR—To Be Regretted—pile. But what must be done has to be done. I'm a survivor-in-training now. I had deleted Tokyo from the weather widget, though.

It seldom snows in Tokyo. You're lucky.

Tokyo.

Sonia.

No more.

#KeepCalm #And #CarryOnWriting

Next > Don't ask and it shall still be given.

Don't ask and it shall still be given.
20 Feb 2016

Rather than menial tasks, Chew had offered a copywriter position. In the meantime, he will be mentoring as I work on the book. Homing us along a land-mine strewn writing journey. I will give it my best. Life owes me nothing. Not at all, really. God has already given me everything. And so, I owe Life instead.

I wasn't expecting all these. They are not just giving me a job. It's a chance. A chance to *live* again. From an unemployee to a copywriter at a top advertising agency. All because I know my bosses. So never lose hope. When hope is thin, remember that the pages in the Bible are thinner than thin. And look at what happened. Whatever can still happen when there is hope. I may be alone. But I'm not lonely anymore. Loneliness is a symptom of getting lost. Purpose is the only treatment, the purpose of Life.

At the hospital, I would gaze at the droplets on the window every morning. The one degree of separation that rivens the world. I may not be able to cross roads but soon, I can transverse worlds. Nothing more I can ask for.

#AloneButTogether

Next > **High that the end is nigh.**

High that the end is nigh.
08 Mar 2016

My days are numbered.

I gently soaped the raggedness. No question about loyalty here. Few things stand by you like a scar. It knows where you've been. But it will never tell. It does not know where you are going. But it'll always be there. Along the way, you may get new scars, but the old ones never leave. They stay to tell a story.

The story of when alone is a place.

I often wonder about my surgery. The device is much bigger than the incision. And how did they wire it to a throbbing heart? Modern medicine is truly amazing. But if it protruded more, I need to say hello to bras faster than you can say Cait Jenner. The device lasts five years. And my bosses had begun raising funds for a better one. When I knew that, I felt relief surge through. If life is a journey, this has been one hell of a ride. Thank you all for hanging on. My days on Lonely Planet are numbered too. The loneliest planet on earth.

Good on me.

#NewBeginning

Next > Memory marks the spot.

Memory marks the spot.
17 Mar 2016

People who say money can't buy happiness have never sat at a cafe on a sunny morning. As part of my cab-riding practice, the therapist brought me to a place I used to frequent. This would have been in our Singapore Coffee Trail. Sipping cautiously, I tried not to break the Rosetta until the very last sip. I love challenges, especially the little ones. Latte art is not just a frivolous pattern on your coffee. It is the culmination of talent and hours of hard work. Great latte art is also a sign that all the steps of coffee making are perfect. I watched the barista whip up a pourover in the spot Sonia and I would have sat. My breath hitched as drops trickled like a magic blossom, ringed by rippling halos. The slow trickling is everything. It gets my coffee rage on. I twirled the spoon though I didn't put sugar. The coffee swirled. And swirled.

Liberating.

Unlike in *SnapChat*, memories have no final resting place in your mind. Favorite hangouts before the stroke had become haunts. Places where teardrops had forgotten they can fall. The heart is also a place. A home away from home. Love is the keeper of keys. Oh, and one last thing.

Where is the lock?

#KeyToHappiness

Next > If not now, when?

38

If not now, when?
01 Apr 2016

Bare your feelings. Do not lock them away.

I shouldered past the door. The moment when memory was all of me. Feeling all the feels. I have three bosses. Lily and Chew and Soo Toon. It feels great to be back. In 2011, I had been late for the interview. I got the time mixed up. *This is surely the last time I'm here,* I thought as I had stepped out. Life, in its strange ways, never quite turns out the way you think it should.

Does it ever.

Chew had said we would find a way to make this work. Knowing him, if we cannot find a way, we will make one. Giving a chance is keeping the promise that life broke. Nothing breaks you more than an unkept promise. But here I am. Not caring a whit about shit. Bowel Malfunction be damned.

Bear your feelings.

Chew coined my return-to-work *NASA re-entry.* How apt. I had been alone in another world. Before I got out from my bath, I caught sight of myself in the mirror. Perfect. Perfectly imperfect. Sonia is happy for me. She knows how much I look forward to be back on the radar.

Dying to live again.

#yaaas

Next > **Who? What? Why? When? Where? How?**

Who? What? Why? When? Where? How?
03 Apr 2016

There is no question. Lily and Chew provided answers long before I had any questions.

Questions of what would I do with Life now. Anguish. Disappointment. Scare. Life after my stroke is a cauldron simmering with emotions. One time Lily's Dad fell critically ill. As a director, I had expected her to cut herself some slack. She didn't. Lily showed up for work as usual, granted she's much less bubbly. Learn to compartmentalize, she had explained. Compartmentalize. Spot on. Put away scattershot feelings and think of what is possible. Whittling down possibilities is easy. There aren't many. Writing, my only talent. Talent is a gift for life. It is a given. The only way you can thank God is to use it to the fullest. And that, for me, is writing a book.

How—

A couple of years before my stroke, Chew and I headed to a cafe for lunch grub. As we left, I swerved for a last look. An A-frame sign had snagged my eyes.

Coffee Drinkers Make Better Lovers.

#LookingBack

Next > **Heavy is the heart that hears the rainbow.**

39

Heavy is the heart that hears the rainbow.
4 Apr 2016

Somewhere over the rainbow. Here for Sonia, here for me.
I broke away and laid down the music box. Love-in-a-box. Every relationship sings a song. This is ours. Over. So not ready for it to be over. Today would have been our fifth anniversary. I am happy we broke up.
Happy for Sonia. Sad for myself. Sadder for us.
The saddest part of breaking up is the unraveling. And you know nothing can stop anything as you watch Love breaks. I had thought of breaking up with Sonia back in 2014. I decided not to. She is a good girl. Sonia deserves a life of no regrets. I wish her well. Nothing salty. I wish Life loves Sonia from this on. Sad is sad, life is life. Sad is bad, life is still life. Life goes on even if you are sad. Do not cling to the past because memories are beautiful. Yesterday will never come again tomorrow. Your being will never be whole again, never, no matter what. Move on.
All goodbyes are hard. The ones unsaid are the hardest. So I asked Sonia how she felt about us. *The right one.* Sonia is certain that she will never meet someone like me again. Always saying what I wanted to tell her.
Never makes perfect.

#LifeFoundEveryWayToEndUs

Next > **When painful and grateful becomes painfully grateful.**

When painful and grateful becomes painfully grateful.
09 Apr 2016

Breathing is a pain. Happy is a feeling. Grateful is when you feel both. I watched, painfully happy, as Sylvester stomped, toting a sippy cup. My body ached madly as my thyroid gland turns underactive after the RAI treatment.
Everyday gives me a lot of pain. Pain, pain and something else. Pain, I think. Pain knows me well.

Especially where it hurts most. Writing adds to it. The pain of remembering. But it is a necessary evil. Remembering is the only way to write on after almost becoming a write-off. My life is based on a true story and I am living a sequel now. One that is worth writing down in a book. Jean-Dominique Bauby was the former editor of *Elle*. He had a massive stroke and ended up locked-in. He could only blink one eyelid. So he wrote his memoir, *The Diving Bell and the Butterfly* by blinking when you recite the correct alphabet. If he had no qualms …

… I have no excuses.

#ChoosePain

Next > **First things last.**

First things last.
18 May 2016

I ran my finger across the page. First draft of the first book I have ever written. Little more than a stack of printouts that Chew had bound. But I am proud. The first cut is always deepest. Stuck for the longest of time, it had been too much of an emotional surrender. Chew provides more than a second pair of eyes. Armed with his wild card—management—he reined me in to get the words out. Writing the blog is cathartic. Writing this book is not. The hurt of what happened. Penned from the GoPro of a man hurtled through the seethe beneath Life. Yet, the last thing I want is to force people to read between the whines. I do not want to end up with a one-way ticket to Snoozeville. This is no vanity project. The book is my way of saying thanks. Anything less would be nothing. Besides, I have pretty much had it with this page of my life. Time to move on.

Let us close this chapter.

#FirstTimeForEverything

Next > **Forget me for remembering us.**

40

Forget me for remembering us.
28 May 2016

*A gentle drizzle is falling when we spot the red arch in
a mist. Kisses stolen by the wind. We follow the swaying
lanterns and approach a water trough. Sonia scoops with
a wooden dipper in her right hand. She pours over the left
hand. She then swaps the dipper to her left hand and pours
over the right. I follow. Next she swigs from a cupped palm
and swishes her mouth. Cleanliness is sacred to Shinto, Sonia
explains. A steady patter grows as we cross the arch again.
Raining is a good omen, she says.*

*How can things be bad? I sneak another glance. Not when
I'm with you, dear.*

Never.

My eyes flicked. Floodlit by blackness. 4:19 a.m.
Writing the book made me think about Sonia and me. A
lot. Tormented by all that I remember, I do not feel painful.
I *am* painful. But never would I give up.

How could I? At a time when I had nothing, Chew
gave me everything. He believed in me. And so I carry on,
no matter what. Hang in there. It gets worse before it gets
better. When your battles get out of hand, fight them on
bended knees.

Pray.

#ThisCouldBeUsButLifePlayin

Next > **Sometimes it ends.**

Sometimes it ends.
01 Jun 2016

I shucked off the pouch. Chew had gotten it for me. He
hooked a carabiner so I can carry things around when my
hands are on the good old crutches. Awesome sauce. One
thing, though. It is capable of holding up to two tons. But
can it bear the weight on my mind?

My world crashed down in one night and is taking years to remake. If career and romance are anything to go, it had been a sugar-coated life. Until running smack into this cut-throat. My first-ever and hopefully last time in forever. No stockpile, I hope. "Will that be all," baristas always ask. Now I ask Life too.

Will that be all?

#OneHitWonder

Next > In good Hands.

In good Hands.
11 Jun 2016

Work gives me a reason to wake up every day. Even on off-days. Gone are the nights too quiet to sleep. Taunted and haunted by moments that shouldn't be remembered. I never imagine being able to work here again after a stroke. Trust God's timing. His watch is perpetual.

I had wondered why things do not work out the way I have wanted. Now I see how they are turning out the way I needed them to. Rock-bottom is the best place to build your life. Because you can only rise. Why do you think broken people come here?

I had always known what I got. I just never knew I would lose them. And I need to write a story about it. A story of when Life taught me Strength 101. Lean on God when it turns dark, even your own shadow leaves.

On rainy mornings when the ground is slippery, I would remember what Brother had told me. How Lily and her husband came down to the ICU and prayed for me. By the time I finish thinking, I would have gotten over to the other side. I may be slow, but I will get there. Going back to work after a stroke is hard. Every. Little. Thing. But my friends' help makes life so much easier. You don't need a reason to help others.

All you need is a chance.

#NoWings #NoHalo #ButAngels

Next > Happy book birthday.

Happy book birthday.
28 Mar 2018

At last, at very last. After 36 months of writing on my phone. Every storyful day. Every wordless night. Everything has come to this.

We are ready for publishing. I am sure the waft of fresh ink would be exciting. One day, this book will be all that is left of me. An aftertaste that lingers long after the coffee is gone.

My stroke did not break my heart only. It broke your boy. And this book pieces my world together. Writing a memoir is real scary. But there is Chew. I had been writing anecdotes on my iPhone (thanks, Steve) and he roped in a bunch of beta readers to give me feedback. The alpha supporters of my life. So I used every word I know to tell the story of a painful time.

A time in memory of when Life forgot.

***

Never is a long time. Though not long enough for me to walk again. Five years after my stroke, I still can't walk. I still can't brew a pourover (Life hates me, still). But maybe one day I can live happily ever after. Maybe even after happily ever after. A definite maybe, I hope.

So there's that. Until then.

See you soon.

#GetReadyWithMe

CREMA SUTRA

1. Maruyama Coffee -
Coffee for the first day of the rest of my life.

2. Sarutahiko Coffee -
Happiness is coffee with you and a good book.

3. Streamer Coffee - In coffee we trust.

4. Lattest Coffee - Girls just wanna have fun!

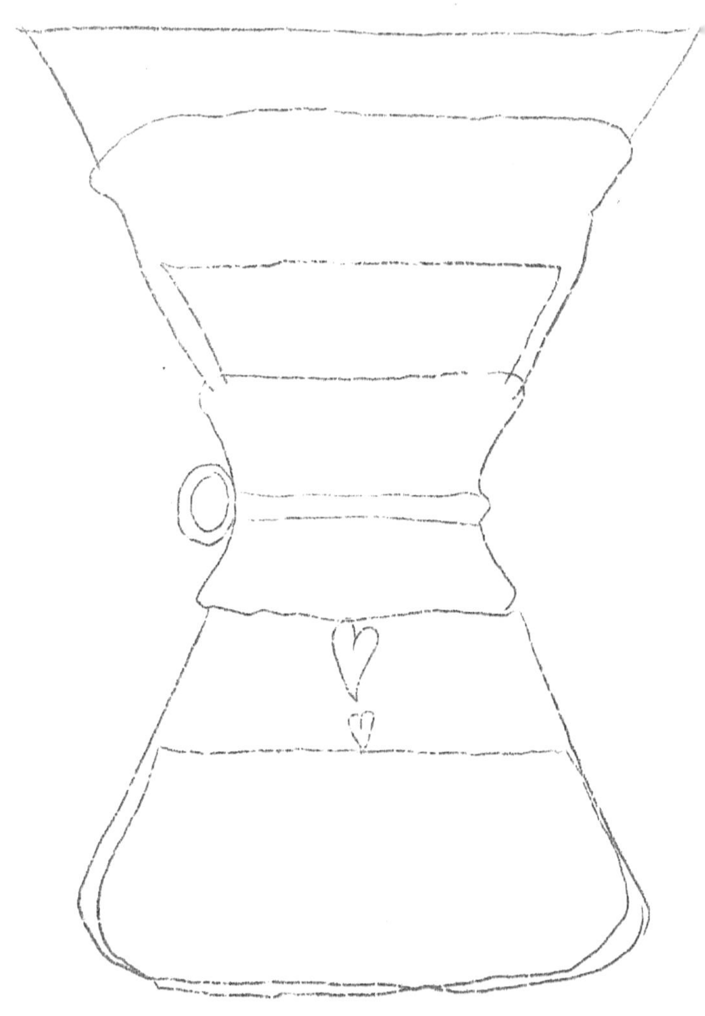

5. Identity Coffee - Kindred spirits? Just follow the coffee.

6. Be A Good Neighbor Coffee - Coffee is our cup of tea.

7. Cafe Legs -
Life is full of storms. Ride it out!

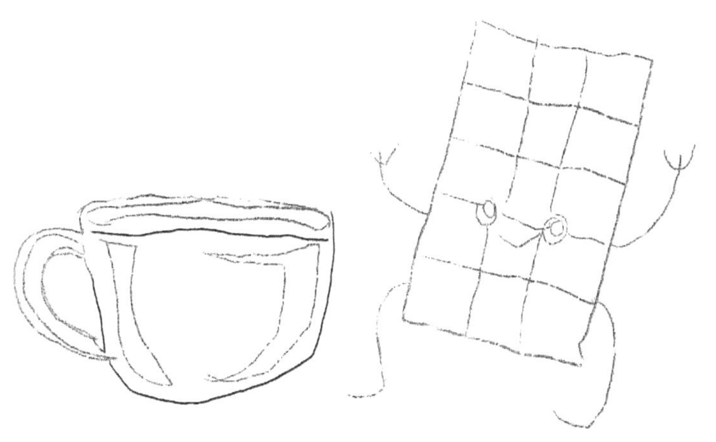

8. Honey Coffee -
Coffee and chocolate. What a time to be alive.

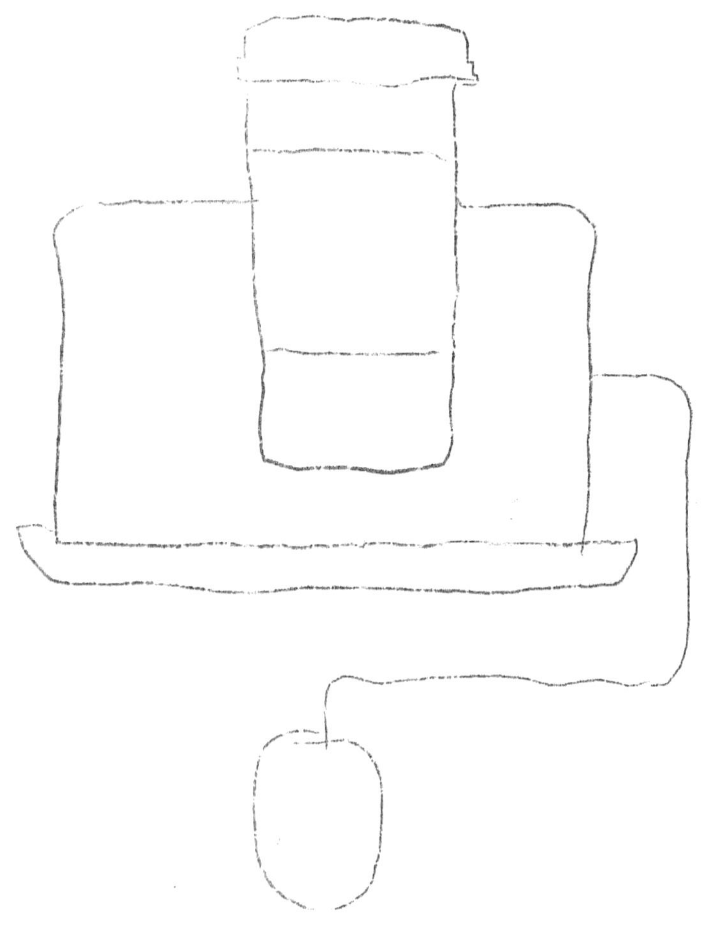

9. The Coffeeshop -
Behind every great design are many cups of coffee.

10. Mocha Coffee - Into the wild.

11. Bear Pond Espresso - Thank you, coffee gods!

12. Little Nap Coffee - Eat, play, love coffee.

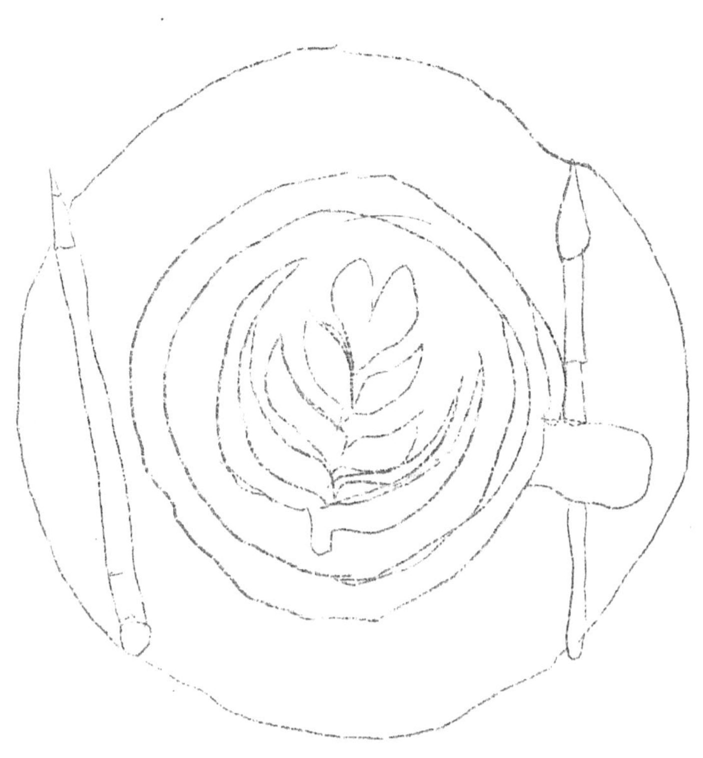

13. Ballon D'essai Latte - Listen to your art.

After

Life can't go on like this.
So I tried.
Harder than ever,
now or never.
I tried to be myself,
tried to be living again.
Even tried to be happy.
But without you,
I can't be.

I just can't be.

THE END

Acknowledgments

Writing a book is hard. Writing this book is harder.
As painful as pain can be. I am eternally grateful to those
who share the pain. As I have no plans for a trilogy, I shall
only put names to people directly involved as I wrote. No
place for everything here. Just more than anything. I will
thank all others with the rest of time.

To Lily Chia:
Thank you for leading me to the Lord. Thank you for
finding me before I got lost. Thank you for teaching me to
begin with the end in mind. Because, as it had turned out,
good things come to an end for better things to begin.

To Chew Lip Heng:
Thank you for believing in me when I believed nothing.
Thank you for suggesting that I write this book. It gave
me a reason to exist. Thank you for guiding me as I wrote.
It gave me a reason to persist. And most importantly,
thank you for all the coffee. It gave me no reason to resist.

To Ho Soo Toon:
Thank you for showing me that life, like golf, goes down
before an upswing. And when you can't be like others,
never give up. You can still play with a handicap.

To the Writers Team at carbon interactive—
Cassandra Sim, Jeng Yi, Jessie Lim, Lavanya
Kannathass, Nadiah Nanni, Sheryl Quek
and Tabitha Tan:
Thank you for learning together. Your ideas have shaped
this into a book that wrote my story. Thanks for editing,
Nad and Tabs. Thanks for coming onboard.

To all folks at carbon interactive and atomz:
Thank you for leading the teams, Jeffrey Lim and
Stephen Chong. With you people around, I don't suffer a
disability. I face one.

To Singapore Civil Defence Force, Farhan the firefighter, Vincent the firebiker, and Pannie the paramedic:
Thank you for letting me see my nephews go Primary One.

To my nurses, doctors, therapists and social workers:
Thank you for holding up my world as I try to
hold on to Life.

To fellow Saints:
Thank you for being wingmen as I fall in love with Life
again. Thank you for hauling my ass off rock-bottom:
Up and On!

To my friends and army mates:
Thank you for the shoulders to lean on (literally).

To Mr Ng Lay Beng:
Thank you for driving me down to work after life drove
me up the wall.

To Amanda Lovelace:
Thank you for the inspiration after my near-expiration.

To Mom and Dad, Brother and Sister-in-law, Sister and my nephews:
Thank you all for being my favorite people in the world.

To my aunts and cousins:
Thank you for being here.

To Sonia:
Thank you for being you.

To me:
Thank you for being me.

To you:
Thank you once more.

And lastly, to God:
Thank you for making our world round so people who are
lost can find themselves.

ABOUT *COFFEE*

Coffee is like no other.

The aroma of a fresh brew is a hug from the mug.
Sweet embrace of every short day and every long night.
Pure bliss. Flecked by luscious bubbles, its acidity sends a
rush of tingles deep into your being. The aftertaste,
languid and soft, lingers like a lucid dream.

No wonder coffee drinkers make better lovers.